Disney World at 50

The Stories of How Walt's Kingdom

Became Magical in Orlando

Orlando Sentinel

TRIUMPH
BOOKS

This book is available in quantity at special discounts for your group or organization. For further information, contact:

Triumph Books LLC
814 North Franklin Street
Chicago, Illinois 60610
Phone: (312) 337-0747
www.triumphbooks.com

Printed in U.S.A.
ISBN: 978-1-62937-982-1
Interior Design by Alex Lubertozzi
Library of Congress Cataloging-in-Publication Data is available upon request

CREDITS
Editorial Team:
Editor—Roger Simmons
Photo Editor—Cassie Armstrong

Orlando Sentinel Media Group:
General Manager—Paul Pham
Editor-in-Chief—Julie Anderson
Managing Editor—Roger Simmons
Content Director/Features—Cassie Armstrong

ON THE COVER
The "Partners" statue by Blaine Gibson, depicting Walt Disney holding the hand of Mickey Mouse, in front of Cinderella Castle at Walt Disney World. This recreation of Gibson's original work at Disneyland was installed at the Magic Kingdom in 1996. Orlando Sentinel photo by Joe Burbank.

All photos courtesy of The Orlando Sentinel unless otherwise indicated.

Contents

Introduction

by Roger Simons, Orlando Sentinel Managing Editor

Like almost every kid growing up in Florida in the late 1960s and early 1970s, I was excited that Mickey Mouse was going to be my neighbor.

I lived in Miami, some 200 miles away from Walt Disney's 27,000-acre property, but I knew what was going on in Orlando. I had some pretty good sources.

First, my grandparents. They lived in Lake County and read the *Orlando Sentinel* every day. In 1965, the *Sentinel* was the first to break the news that Walt Disney was coming to Central Florida. The newspaper's many stories have kept readers and residents up to date about the happenings at Walt Disney World for decades. As the Magic Kingdom was being built, my grandparents would tell me all about what they learned from the *Sentinel*.

My second source (because good journalists always need two!) was my father. He was a truck driver who hauled construction equipment from South Florida to "Disney"—the term we in-the-know Floridians used as shorthand for Walt Disney World. While dropping off bulldozers, road graders, and other vehicles, my dad would get information from the construction workers to share with us.

He'd tell us stories about 20,000 Leagues Under the Sea ("They're having a rough time with that one," Dad said, shaking his head), or about the Contemporary Hotel with its module-style rooms ("It's all made of steel—no chance of a fire doing much damage there," he said in amazement).

After hearing all about Disney World for what seemed like forever, I finally got to see it for myself when I was seven years old. My dad, younger brother Craig, and I drove up to Orlando.

We spent a full day in the park riding the monorail (that was cool), visiting the Haunted Mansion (it scared my brother; I wasn't afraid!), and going on Eastern Airlines' If You Had Wings (I still have that ride's song stuck in my head) and 20,000 Leagues (of course!). As we were leaving, my dad let each of us get souvenirs. I picked a Mickey MousekeEars hat; my brother chose a beanie with a propeller and a Mickey Mouse balloon.

We left the park and drove to my grandparents' house to spend the night. My brother and I, worn out by the big day, slept most of the short car ride. As soon as we got out of the car, my grandmother took one look at us, then turned to my dad and asked, "When did Roger and Craig get chicken pox?"

Yes, years before a global pandemic, on my first trip to Disney World, I was either a superspreader or just unlucky.

Which brings us to today. I doubt Walt ever envisioned that the 50th anniversary of his grand "Florida Project" would be taking place amid the COVID-19 crisis. But, as they say in the entertainment world, the show must go on.

We hope you enjoy this book filled with stories and pictures produced over the decades by *Orlando Sentinel* reporters and photographers about the world's most popular tourist attraction.

Because, 50 years later, we're still Mickey's neighbors. 🐭

The iconic view of Cinderella Castle (facing page) has been greeting visitors to Walt Disney World's Magic Kingdom since 1971. This photo was taken shortly after the theme park opened by Central Florida resident Sibyl Brown, grandmother to Orlando Sentinel *managing editor Roger Simmons.*

CHAPTER 1

The Big Mystery in Florida

In 1965, secret sales of huge swaths of land were taking place in Central Florida, and the rumors about who the buyer might be were as plentiful as the scrub palmetto on the property. It took *Orlando Sentinel* "girl reporter" Emily Bavar (yes, that's really how the newspaper identified her in a front-page headline back then) to break the biggest story in the region's history: Walt Disney, the man with the famous movie studio and wildly popular Disneyland theme park, was coming to town. When he did arrive in Orlando to share his vision for his "Florida Project," he was a little vague about details.

Facing page: Walt Disney (in white) and William "Joe" Potter, a retired U.S. Army general who worked for Disney, spent years secretly purchasing more than 27,000 acres of Central Florida property. Here they are seen touring their real estate.

The Big Mystery in Florida

Walt's Secret Scouting Trip

October 1, 1971 | Dick Marlow, Orlando Sentinel

It was the summer of 1965 when a pleasant visitor signed the registry "Bill Davis" at a Silver Springs motel and checked in unceremoniously for a brief stay.

To the desk clerk he was just another tourist eager to take a look at the catfish through the glass-bottom boats of Silver Springs.

Or he might have been an out-of-town horseman looking over the stock at Ocala Stud Farm.

But the "Bill Davis" shown on the registry was Walt Disney—a dreamer who spent a lifetime making his dreams come true.

Bay Lake, with its island that Walt Disney said reminded him of Tom Sawyer's, drew his attention to this property. Facing page: Disney and Potter inspect the property that will become the home of Disney World.

With him on the trip were several high-ranking Disney executives, including Jack Sayers, now vice president of industry sales for Walt Disney Productions.

"Bill David was a *nom de plume* Walt liked to use on such trips," said Sayers as he recalled the mission, kept secret to hold down real estate prices.

Disney first looked at a rolling spread of land near Ocala "near a horse farm."

It was rejected. Too small.

Next, the task force looked at land near Silver Springs.

According to Sayers,

Disney had come to Florida seeking a site for the most ambitious undertaking of his illustrious career—a theme park complete with five hotels and Epcot, an experimental futuristic city that never stops building the second phase of the Disney dream.

"Walt didn't like it at all."

"He wanted a bigger piece of land," said Sayers. "Another factor was the weather. It really gets cold up there."

The following day, the group was flying over Central Florida in a company plane.

Walt Disney, William Potter (mostly obscured), Roy Disney, Card Walker, and an unidentified man look over maps of Central Florida land purchased for Walt Disney World's new theme park.

"We were over this big lake," said Sayers. "Walt looked down, spotted an island in the lake, and said, 'There's Tom Sawyer's Island. Buy it.'"

It was Bay Lake, now the site of the vast 1,057-room Contemporary Resort Hotel just three minutes away from the theme park entrance by the monorail that whisks guests through the enormous open mall lobby on the way to the park.

The property was bought and the rumor mill cranked up. 🐭

An aerial of the more than 27,000 acres of Disney World property before construction begins. Bay Lake is in the lower left corner.

Walt: "A Great Actor but a Terrible Liar"

October 1, 1971 | Emily Bavar, Orlando Sentinel

Walt Disney, the man who built an empire on a mouse, seemed quiet to the point of shyness as we were ushered into his august presence.

True, he looked the part of a motion picture tycoon; handsome, trim, tanned. He wore light blue slacks, a blue herringbone sport coat and a blue Windsor scarf knotted with careless care.

Conservative by today's standards, but this was 1965 and men's fashions had not yet outgrown their somber hues.

I was with a group of five southern newspaper writers invited to California to tour Disneyland.

But more important to our group than escorted tours of the fabled Disneyland was the scheduled meeting and lunch with Walt Disney. I was, as usual, the only woman among the writers, a fact of life I had grown accustomed to. And as the press conference opened, I silently rehearsed a question I had been reserving for Disney.

For months, adjourning parcels of pasture, swamp and wild acreage near Orlando and Kissimmee had been quietly purchased by a Miami concern for an unknown client.

As the purchases grew to thousands of acres, speculation rose to the point of frenzy.

It was McDonnell Aircraft, some said with conviction. It was David Rockefeller said others. Or Howard Hughes. Or Walt Disney. Or several companies joined forces on the Manned Orbiting Laboratory project.

Was Walt Disney the buyer of the mystery acreage in Orange and Osceola Counties?

I put the question to him and watched for his reaction— any sign that would betray him. There was none.

In retrospect I can credit Walt Disney with an acting talent equal to his artistic genius. He dismissed the question with a shrug and moved to the next.

I felt as subtle as Minnie Mouse as I bombarded this man with questions he clearly didn't wish to answer. I sat beside him at lunch and was certain I was ruining his lamb chops as I turned the

Disney had cemented himself as a giant of American entertainment with his movie studio and Disneyland theme park. He started looking for an east coast location for another theme park venture—and doggone it—found the perfect spot in Central Florida. Photo courtesy of AP Images

Orlando Sentinel *reporter Emily Bavar poses with Disney at a 1965 meeting near Disneyland. In 1965, she wrote the story revealing that the Walt Disney Co. was the mystery industry buying land in Orange County.*

conversation from Disneyland back to Central Florida, a subject on which he finally began to display amazing knowledge.

He knew the average annual rainfall, he was familiar with present and proposed highways, he knew there would be a large labor force available as work on Cape Kennedy tapered off.

Walt Disney was a great actor but a terrible liar.

When I returned to my hotel room that evening I went over my notes. He hadn't said yes, but he hadn't said no. And he knew far more about Central Florida than many of us who have lived here most of our lives.

The Central Florida acreage had to be Walt Disney's. That's what I told my editor when I called him from the Disneyland Hotel in Anaheim.

And that's what we told *Orlando Sentinel* readers the next morning. 🐭

"Girl Reporter" Makes a Bold Prediction

October 21, 1965 | Emily Bavar, Orlando Sentinel

Orange County's 30,000-acre mystery industry site may turn out to be an aircraft testing ground, an electronics research center, or even a washing machine factory.

But I predict nothing so mundane for the mystery site.

I predict it will be an extension of Walt Disney's magic empire of fiction, fantasy, and enormous wealth.

In sticking out my neck with such indifference to caution, I'll go even farther and say the ultimate plan for the spread of acreage is something that could be hatched only in the fertile Disney imagination; that it will be worth watching and waiting for.

I have talked only to Walt Disney who...did not say he had bought the property.

But neither did he say he had *not* bought it.

In talking to Disney it became immediately apparent he had watched the eastern United States with interest and speculation.

Though he underestimated the population of Florida by several million, Disney was familiar with Florida tourist figures, the activity around Cape Kennedy, and the scenic Central Florida area centered by Orlando.

He mentioned Crystal River and expressed a sentimental interest in Daytona Beach where his parents lived early in their marriage. He offered climate and population reasons why Florida would be unacceptable as a site for an amusement park and then showed how these same reasons could be overcome. Yet Walt Disney's plans for expanding his empire would not necessarily stop at another Disneyland.

"There is only *one* Disneyland," he said. Then, almost but not quite as an afterthought, he added, "as such." 🐭

Big Ideas for Florida but Not a Lot of Details

November 16, 1965 | Elvis Lane, Orlando Sentinel

Walt Disney, an artist with the greatest of imaginations, left a lot to the imagination.

Walt Disney, Gov. Burns, Roy Disney Preside At Conference

But these facts did emerge during his visit to Orlando: the Disney entertainment project in Orange and Osceola Counties will be bigger and better than California's Disneyland.

It will cost more than $100 million to prepare it, and it will employ 4,000 persons.

Also, there are to be two incorporated communities in the Disney project, one to be named "Tomorrow" and the other "Yesterday."

The Disney entertainment center will be "fresh and unique," but it will not be called Disneyland.

Disney added that at present he has no idea what his new entertainment attraction will be called. But it will be much bigger than Disneyland was when it started, he agreed.

"It has to be," he explained. The public will expect that from Disney Productions, he added.

At the first meeting, which jam-packed the Cherry Plaza's Egyptian Room, Disney told that he had considered many other sites before deciding on Florida.

The audience at the first meeting estimated from 400 to 500 persons kept waiting for Disney to be specific about what he planned to build.

And newsmen at the press conference tried to pin him down. He still spoke in generalities.

He finally admitted that whatever he planned for Central Florida "might be completed" within three years from now.

Disney stressed how much planning must be done, how many creative people are involved, and "all this takes time."

Disney talked glowingly of the future but evaded whether his project or projects would be a "City of Tomorrow."

True, he later said that one of his communities will be named "Tomorrow." But, he explained, such a city might be outdated before construction is finished.

Disney has thought for sometime about a model city, he admitted. 🐭

In November 1965, Walt Disney, William Potter, Florida Gov. Haydon Burns, and Roy Disney held a press conference in the Egyptian Room at the Cherry Plaza in Orlando. Disney announced plans for what would become Disney World.

Name Game:
It's Disney World

December 22, 1965 | Ed Hensley,
Orlando Sentinel

Tallahassee—Walt Disney's $100 million-plus venture in Central Florida will be known as Disney World and will feature a city of yesterday and a city of tomorrow.

This is not official, but it was the firm conviction Tuesday of state comptroller Fred O. (Bud) Dickinson Jr., who has just returned from Anaheim, California, with a team of other state officials, from a conference with high officials of Disney Enterprises and Disney himself.

Dickinson made this prediction at a press conference here Tuesday to report on his conferences with Disney officials on his four-day visit to the California city.

Dickinson said Disney was most anxious to get started on his Florida project in Orange and Osceola counties on a 27,500-acre tract of land he has purchased. 🐭

Walt Disney, William Potter, and Roy Disney (from left to right) all had key roles in the acquisition and development of what would become Walt Disney World.

Fred Dickinson Convinced

The Name: Disney World

By ED HENSLEY
Sentinel Tallahassee Bureau

TALLAHASSEE—Walt Disney's $100 million plus venture in Central Florida will be known as Disney World and will feature a city of yesterday and a city of tomorrow.

This is not official, but it was the firm conviction Tuesday of State Comptroller Fred O. (Bud) Dickinson Jr., who has just returned from Anaheim, Calif., with a team of other state officials, from a conference with high officials of Disney Enterprises and Disney himself.

DICKINSON made this prediction at a press conference here Tuesday to report on his conferences with Disney officials on his four-day visit to the California city.

Dickinson said Disney was most

Osceola counties on a 27,500-acre tract of land he has purchased.

The comptroller said that Disney officials are coming to Florida in mid-January for another series of conferences on taxes and other issues. These conferences will be held here in Tallahassee.

DICKINSON emphasized that the Disney interests are asking no tax concessions from Florida.

"We are not asking any special concessions," he quoted Roy Disney, business manager, as saying.

"There will be no special concessions," the comptroller said. "We stand to gain far more by working with them, not by giving concessions."

DICKINSON said the state would treat the Disney interests as it would any other industry coming into Florida.

CHAPTER 2

Walt Plans to Change the World

Walt Disney viewed his vast Florida property as the place to build a different kind of world. He wanted to create a "city of tomorrow," a reimagining of America's urban centers that could serve as a template for the future. He called his plan the Experimental Prototype Community of Tomorrow and even made a film to explain his vision. But when it was shown to the public just months after Walt's death in December 1966, company officials explained that Disney World had changed. Epcot was moved to the backburner. "We feel that we can build an attraction here that will bring traffic and tourists and the rest can come later," Roy Disney, Walt's brother, said. As construction started in Florida, the Disney company began shifting its focus to creating what it would call "Vacation Kingdom" and "Theme Park." It would certainly not be the Epcot Walt imagined, but it would become "the most magical place on Earth."

Facing page: This brochure, released to the media in 1969 by Walt Disney Productions, gave more details about what to expect at Walt Disney World. A number of notable planned attractions were included.

Cinderella's Castle — entrance to Fantasyland

Western River Expedition —
Frontierland

"THE MAGIC KINGDOM"

About the same size as California's Disneyland, the new "Magic Kingdom" will include seven lands whose themes are yesterday, tomorrow, adventure, history and storybook classics. Some attractions will be familiar to the 79 million people who have visited California's Disneyland. But many more — like the attractions pictured on these pages — will be new and unique to this new theme park in Walt Disney World.

Thunder Mesa — Frontierland

Epcot: "A New, Different Kind of World"

October 26, 1966 | Norma Lee Browning, Orlando Sentinel via Chicago Tribune

Hollywood—The new Disney World near Orlando, most ambitious project of Walt Disney's vast empire, has progressed well beyond the gleam-in-the-eye stage. And it's not going to be just a Florida-based Disneyland.

"It's going to be a world, a new, different kind of world," said the genius creator who has brought so much joy and laughter to the world.

But this isn't enough. Now he's bringing us Epcot, a city of some 30,000 inhabitants. Epcot stands for "Experimental Prototype Community of Tomorrow." What's it like?

"It's like the city of tomorrow ought to be." said Walt Disney, "A city that caters to the people as a service function. It will be a planned, controlled community, a showcase for American industry

and research, schools, cultural and educational opportunities.

"In Epcot there will be no slum areas because we won't let them develop.

"There'll be no landowners, and therefore no voting control. People will rent homes instead of buying them, and at modest rentals. There will be no retirees. Everyone must be employed. One of our requirements is that the people who live in Epcot must help keep it alive," Disney said.

Epcot is only one of two prototype cities planned for Florida's Disney World. The other, which hasn't been named yet, will be a city built specifically as an experimental laboratory for administering municipal governments. Retirees or others who wish to buy property can buy in this city, but not in Epcot, said Disney.

But isn't Disney World going to have a Disneyland?

"Oh, you betcha," said Walt. "And it's going to be bigger than the one here. We are not going to disappoint the Florida tourists."

Why did he choose Florida for Disney World? And especially Orlando?

A photo of the original design for Walt Disney's Epcot, which included a central skyscraper with a city laid out around the central business and entertainment district. This picture came from Kent Tripp, from a photo album that belonged to his grandfather, General Joe Potter. Potter was instrumental in the construction of Walt Disney World and Disneyland.

"Florida and Southern California are the only two places where you can count on the tourists," he said. "I don't like ocean sites because of the beach crowd, and also the ocean limits the approach. If you'll notice, Disneyland at Anaheim is like a hub with freeways converging on it from all sides....That's why we chose Orlando.

"There are literally millions of Disneyland addicts, I'm sure, who simply will never believe that another Disney World in Florida, or any other place, can possibly measure up to the magic world in Anaheim.

"But I've got a lot more room to play with," said Walt, with a sparkle in his eye.

Having major roads nearby was an important factor in the selection of the Orlando area for Disney's Florida Project. This 1965 photo shows Interstate 4 construction through downtown Orlando.

Famous Showman Passes, but Walt's Project Will Go Forward

December 16, 1966 | Don Rider, Orlando Sentinel

A sorrowing Central Florida was assured Thursday that plans for Disneyland East will be carried forward.

The untimely death of Walt Disney had touched off speculation the future of the major tourist attraction he proposed for this area was in jeopardy.

However, Jim Stewart, spokesman for the Disney enterprises, told the *Sentinel*: "Previous to Mr. Disney's first entering the hospital for his operation, he clearly and in great detail delineated to the organization his plans and dreams for the individual elements of his Florida project.

The news of Walt Disney's death shocked the world, especially Central Florida.

"It is the determination of Roy Disney, the Disney family, and the entire Disney organization that these plans be carried forward."

Roy Disney, older brother, chairman of the board, and president of Walt Disney Productions, went further.

He said: "All of the plans for the future that Walt had begun—new motion pictures, the expansion of Disneyland, television production, and our Florida and Mineral King projects—will continue to move ahead. That is the way Walt wanted it to be."

Disney (left) receives a commendation from the from Dr. H.C. Niese, Argentine consul at Los Angeles, in 1933. Disney (right) poses at the Pancoast Hotel in Miami in 1941. He knew a lot about Florida from his parents, who were married in Lake County and later lived in Daytona Beach. Photo courtesy of AP Images

A Change in Plans for Disney's World

February 3, 1967 | Don Rider, Orlando Sentinel

Epcot is the project that captured Disney's imagination, but it will not be first in development, or even in the first stage. His brother, Roy, president and chairman of the board of Walt Disney Productions, revealed the change in planning.

Roy Disney said the theme park, similar but five times larger than Disneyland at Anaheim, will be built first.

"We believe if we get eight to 12 million customers there, it will be a lot easier to attract industry."

From south to north, the layout on Disney World will be: jet airport in Osceola County, an entrance complex with parking for 11,000 cars, a 1,000-acre industrial park to be a showcase for new ideas, then Epcot, and on the far north, the amusement park.

Florida Gov. Claude Kirk (left) reacts during a news conference in which Roy Disney (right) made public for the first time details about the new Disney World complex before hundreds of travel editors and Florida businessmen on February 2, 1967.

Shifting Focus to the New "Theme Park"

February 12, 1967 | Emily Bavar, Orlando Sentinel

What in the world (Disney World, of course), is a Theme Park?

Loaded questions such as this are designed to carry reporters to journalistic peaks, and when properly aimed, results are sometimes startling.

For example: "A Theme Park," Disney Productions vice president Donn Tatum explained with patience, "is a park with a theme." The Disney World Theme Park will have eight themes, all built

Roy Disney (above, foreground), William Potter, and others visit the island in the middle of Bay Lake during their February 4, 1967, inspection of the Disney property. Disney, Potter, and others (below) survey a map spread out on the hood of a car on the same day.

E. Cardon Walker, William Potter, Don Tatum and Roy Disney (from left to right) inspect their Florida property before the building of Disney World on February 4, 1967.

in a circular pattern around a central amusement park.

There will be a frontierland, Polynesian, Cape Cod, Dutch, African, and Asian villages; a Spanish Colonial settlement of early California style and a City of Yesterday.

Each of these attractions will open with 750 motel rooms, a convention center, shops, restaurants, recreation and entertainment areas, all in harmony with its own theme. Each will overlook the amusement park and the neighboring theme villages. So, if you happen to be a guest on the Polynesian Island and find appeal in the Cape Cod village, you can stroll over for a New England boiled dinner.

The entire amusement park will cover around 1,000 acres on the shore of Bay Lake which will be enlarged, the muck dredged from its sand bottom and weeds cleared from its beach.

Originally, there was talk of an African animal conservation attraction for Reedy Creek, which flows from Bay Lake, but there's nothing definite on that yet. Donn Tatum thinks Reedy Creek is a magnificent setting for animals to roam free in natural surroundings and it may someday be used for that purpose. Meanwhile, it will be preserved much as it is right now—its towering trees and tropical vegetation protecting the birds and animals that live there.

The Disney people want to make the park important enough to bring people here to see it, complete enough to take care of them while they're here, and entertaining enough to make the trip worthwhile. 🐭

Now It's the Vacation Kingdom

January 11, 1968 | Jack McDavitt, Orlando Sentinel

Walt Disney World Co., which announced it will move its administrative staff here next month, will spend nearly $17 million this year preparing for the 1971 opening of Disney World and its "vacation kingdom."

And, company officials said, the first phase of the 27,400-acre, $500 million project will indeed be a "vacation kingdom."

The center of the kingdom will be the Disney World amusement park, which will include such attractions as a "Bear Band," "Hall of Presidents," "Colonial America Land," and "Space Mountain."

But, company officials said, the amusement area will be "just one of many entertainment and recreation attractions" available on opening day, January 1, 1971.

Unlike California's Disneyland, the hotels and motels here will be part of Disney World and will be resorts, not just rooms, officials said.

In addition, Disney officials said, the opening phase calls for "extension and enlargement of Bay Lake, a natural body of water, into a three-mile waterway dotted with natural and man-made islands.

Central Florida business leaders and Disney executives gather to review a huge model of the Walt Disney World property and hear a presentation on the company's plans for its theme park development.

A COMPLETE EDITION ABOUT

Walt Disney World

"The Vacation Kingdom of the World"

This 1969 brochure predicted what Walt Disney World might look like in a few years, with the Magic Kingdom and several hotels built around the Seven Seas Lagoon and Bay Lake.

In its new form, it will become the focus of water spectacles and sports, while at the same time retaining its original, often spectacular beauty.

"In essence, then, at its opening in 1971, Walt Disney World will present a complete 'vacation kingdom,' a place of entertainment crowned by a new and different Disneyland, a place of entertainment where land and water sports abound, and a place of relaxation catering to the needs not only of the guest who comes for the day, but planned and oriented around activities and adventures for those who stay here for part or all of their family vacation," the company said.

Overseeing this work will be William E. Potter, Disney vice president in charge of Disney World development, who will move permanently to Orlando next month. 🐭

Persian

Located on the lake, the Persian-style hotel will create the effect of visiting an exotic far eastern palace. Crowning the central lobby will be a colossal dome, from which balconies will radiate to the 500 rooms. Accommodations will look out over the lake or onto beautifully landscaped courtyards.

Asian

The Asian-style hotel is primarily Thai in its decor and food specialties. Two-thirds of its 600 rooms are planned "on the water" or in garden settings — the remainder will be in a 160-foot high tower building, overlooking the lagoon and a central recreation area. All convention facilities will be underneath and separated from the main public areas.

Venetian

In the style of St. Mark's Square, the 500-room Venetian theme resort will be strongly oriented to water activities. It will feature an enclosed small boat harbor, entered from the lagoon area, and an intricate system of water-ways designed to create the atmosphere of Venice. The glass-topped lobby will produce a sunny atrium effect indoors.

Original plans for Disney World in 1969 included several hotels that would be built in the first five years of the opening of the Magic Kingdom. But the 600-room Asian, 500-room Persian, and 500-room Venetian hotels were never constructed.

THE THEME RESORTS

A journey 'round the World

The charm of old Europe and the romance of South
Islands is just a monorail ride away inside the Vaca
Kingdom of Walt Disney World. This time, stay in
world of tomorrow at the Contemporary-style hotel.
your next visit, step back in time into the splendo
an Asian palace. Imagine the fun of a family holida

Polynesian

*The place to stay for sports
enthusiasts — the Polynesian-
theme hotel. There's a special
pool for scuba-diving . . . golf
nearby at the Walt Disney World
courses . . . and boating almost at
your doorstep. One-third of the
rooms are planned for the graceful high-rise structure — and all
700 rooms will face the water.*

DISNEY WORLD *at* 50

Contemporary

lagship" of the theme resorts
Walt Disney World is the
0-room Contemporary-style
tel. Walt Disney World-Alweg
onorail trains will travel
rectly through its 80-foot high
en mall "lobby," ringed by
ops, cafes and restaurants.
ajor conventions will head-
arter here and use its grand
llroom; exhibit rooms and
eeting rooms.

a family-oriented convention — with all the attrac-
ns of the new "Magic Kingdom" *plus* boating, water
ing, swimming, golf, tennis, moonlight cruises on
e lake, theatre shows and hotel night club entertain-
nt. It's all coming to the world's new vacation capi-
Walt Disney World, beginning October, 1971.

In 1969, the Contemporary was described as the "flagship" of the theme resorts at Walt Disney World, while the Polynesian was called, "the place to stay for sports enthusiasts."

CHAPTER 3

Building the Magic Kingdom

Just weeks before the U.S. would send the first humans to the moon's surface, another truly American endeavor was preparing for launch. Final plans were unveiled for the Magic Kingdom at Disney World, and construction was well underway. Like the moon mission, the building of Mickey's Florida home would involve new technology and innovative construction techniques. As the countdown clock started for a planned October 1, 1971, opening, Disney would keep the public updated on the theme park construction by opening a Preview Center—and it would become a tourist attraction unto itself, attracting more than 1 million visitors.

Facing page: A welder works on the construction of a restaurant in Walt Disney World's Magic Kingdom near Orlando in this undated photo. In the background is Cinderella Castle, which will be the focal point of phase one of the amusement park, scheduled to open in 1971.

Making the Disney World Dream a Reality

May 1, 1969 | Ormund Powers, Orlando Sentinel

Four of the nation's industrial giants will join forces in Walt Disney World's $165 million Vacation Kingdom, the nation's press was told at a glittering unveiling Wednesday.

RCA, United States Steel, the Monsanto Co. and Aerojet General Corp. will cooperate in revolutionary construction methods for the giant tourist attraction, scheduled to open 15 miles southwest of Orlando in October 1971.

U.S. Steel will build two hotels, one a contemporary A-frame building of 10 stories, the other a 12-story Polynesian-style resort.

Together they will have 1,450 rooms, all to be built of steel on the ground, assembled and furnished on the ground, then hauled by derrick, connected by an ingenious interlock system, and the utilities plugged in.

RCA will install a total information communications system for guests, residents,

A view of the dock and teen swimming pool in Bay Lake at Walt Disney World, being built near Orlando, Florida, July 7, 1971.

and management. Guests will be able to receive personal television bulletins, and there will be continuous electronic tracking of events throughout the widespread Vacation Kingdom.

News and previews of Walt Disney World activities will be available continuously through hotel room television and sets in other locations. Closed-circuit systems will train new employees and monitor shows and attractions.

Aerojet General will install what could be the ultimate answer to air pollution and garbage disposal in cities: a complete underground system of pneumatic tubes that will transport all garbage and trash, dirty hotel linen and the like to a central point for handling.

This will eliminate garbage cans, garbage trucks and the nuisance associated with them.

Monsanto will develop a large exhibit in the Theme Park and has assigned one of its executives

Main Street, U.S.A. at the Magic Kingdom under construction at Walt Disney World prior to the opening of the Florida theme park in 1971.

to work full-time with Disney people so the latest technology, research, and enterprise of the firm can be utilized in the project development.

"Vacation Kingdom," an exceptional approach to family holidays, is the goal of the Disney people, the press audience heard and applauded Wednesday.

For the kids there will be the Disneyland-type amusements and attractions, most of them different from those in Anaheim, California. There

Walt Disney World is under construction near Orlando in Central Florida
July 7, 1971. At center is the amusement park's Cinderella Castle.

Building the Magic Kingdom

Workers continue to build the City Hall on Main Street, U.S.A. as they rush to get the Magic Kingdom ready for its opening day.

The nearly $500 million family-oriented complete vacation center veers away from Disneyland in Anaheim, which is essentially a place you go to spend a day or two to see the shows and exhibits and enjoy the rides.

Disney World will be different, the only thing of its kind in the world, as is typical of Disney thinking and planning.

In this vast endeavor, 27,000 acres of Florida scrub land will become a dream area, a place of superb beauty and fascination for those of all ages.

The magnitude of "Vacation Kingdom" can be grasped better if you spend an hour or two touring the site—twice the size of Manhattan Island in New York—as the 200 press, radio, television, and magazine writers and editors from throughout the world did.

The Disney people have already moved 4.2 million cubic yards of dirt. Essentially, they are rearranging the earth on their property, creating 55 miles of canals and a huge man-made lagoon, deepening Bay Lake, building raised earth foundations for the many structures.

They have pumped up nearly four miles of white sand beach around Bay Lake. Soon they will pump the lake dry, clean it, and refill it and the channels and lagoons with clear, fresh water.

More than 200 pieces of heavy equipment have been used in this enormous land alteration program, a program so huge in scope that much of it has been carried out at night, illumination provided workers by brilliant portable spotlights.

But that phase is about finished. Soon, the pouring of concrete, the erection of steel, and

will be swimming, boating, skin-diving, horse-riding nature trails, bicycling, archery, and tennis.

For the adults there will be all these things plus golf on three magnificent courses, live theater and movies, and five luxurious hotels all with different motifs with music, dancing, exotic foods, and entertainment.

Eastern seaboard-style architecture from turn-of-the-century America is being recreated on Main Street, U.S.A. at Walt Disney World's Magic Kingdom in November 1970.

Building the Magic Kingdom

The Contemporary Resort Hotel, under construction at Walt Disney World, on July 7, 1971.

the sawing and nailing of boards will begin, as well as the replanting of the 8,000 trees of all varieties, from all corners of the world—including Redwoods from California—now nestled in the project's vast tree farm.

Walt Disney loved trees, and not a single tree or bush has been destroyed or moved unless it was absolutely necessary. Much of the terrain remains covered with pines, cypress, palmetto, scrub oak, all the things dear to Floridians and will remain so.

Guests arriving at Vacation Kingdom by car—about 80 percent of the first year's 8 million—will park in a lot accommodating 14,000 vehicles, then go into the area via either double-deck, side-wheeler boats, surface transportation, or one of the six five-car monorail trains.

There they will see a complete vacationland, the new Magic Kingdom theme park with some of the attractions familiar to the 79 million people who have already visited Disneyland in California, but many more unique.

A few steps away from the entrance, which is also the transportation center, guests will be departing for a grand circle tour around the Magic Kingdom aboard old-fashioned trains of the Walt Disney World railroad.

Inside the Magic Kingdom, visitors, as Roy Disney outlines, "will literally bridge time and theme when they step into its seven realms—Main Street, Adventureland, Frontierland, Fantasyland, Tomorrowland, Liberty Square and Holidayland."

Some of the new concepts being created by Walt E. Disney Enterprises for its Florida project include Thunder Mesa, a spectacular panorama of the Old West.

Space Mountain will be 20 stories tall, embracing a number of adventures and attractions themed to the world of the future in Tomorrowland.

Liberty Square will recreate America's past at the time of our nation's founding, where shops and stores will portray life in Colonial days.

Country Bear Band will be a foot-stomping country and western hoedown by animated bears.

The Mickey Mouse Musical Revue will be a visit with 60 of the famous characters from the Disney films.

Western River Expedition will be a musical parody of the wild Old West, in which boat-riding explorers come face-to-face with cowboys and Indians in a frontier fantasy.

One Nation Under God will be an inspiring dramatization about the American Constitution and the 37 presidents.

In addition to the two hotels being built by U.S. Steel, there will be the Persian, Venetian, and Asian theme resort hotels to follow. In all, there will be 4,000 hotel and motel rooms, a convention center accommodating 2,000 persons for meetings, 1,500 for dinners, plus 10,000 square feet of exhibit space and eight smaller meeting rooms. There will be many restaurants offering a variety of American, European, and Asian foods.

Disney World Preview Center Delights All

January 17, 1970 | Charlie Wadsworth, Orlando Sentinel

Neither fog nor rain could stay the steady stream of visitors as they poured into Walt Disney World's Preview Center, which opened to the public Friday.

They came. They saw. They were conquered.

Despite heavy fog and rain, more than 3,000 eager people—who had awaited the opportunity for a peek at the entertainment bonanza—came and were awed at the informative presentation.

Mr. and Mrs. B. A. McMillan and son, Scott, came to town on business from Omaha, Nebraska. They stayed over in Orlando Thursday night so they could visit the center before going to St. Petersburg.

"I liked it very much. I will have lots to say to our friends in Omaha who want to know about this," said Mrs. McMillan.

"I was very much impressed," her husband added.

"I thought it was neat," said 13-year-old Scott.

Guests went to a registration counter where hostesses had them sign under the guest's home state.

Then it was to the film room for a look at the 650-square-foot model of Walt Disney World and a 12-minute film telling how the late Walt Disney dreamed up WDW and what it will be like.

Guests then wandered through the $500,000 center, looking at up-to-date construction

progress pictures, artists' renderings of shows to be held at the entertainment complex, and models of the huge hotels to be built near the center.

The hostesses had been in training for several weeks prior to the opening.

The Disney World Preview Center opened at Lake Buena Vista on January 10, 1970, and closed on September 30, 1971, the day before Disney World opened.

And a week before Friday's opening, Disney invited transportation, rental car, and public officials from all over the state to acquaint them with the project.

But these same officials received a few surprises themselves. TV and movie star Buddy Ebsen, in his hometown on a visit, casually wandered in for a "looksee." He was, he said, completely "fascinated by it all."

The preview center was built to inform guests what Walt Disney World is going to be and what has been going on at the project site for the past two years.

There is no admission charge, and the center will be open seven days a week from 9:00 AM to 5:00 PM. 🐭

Cars line up outside the Disney World Preview Center in January 1970. The free attraction gave visitors a peek at what the Magic Kingdom would become.

CHAPTER 4

Opening Day Finally Arrives

Six years after Walt Disney purchased 27,800 acres of land for this Florida fantasy, the gates finally opened at the Magic Kingdom on October 1, 1971. Officials worried about a repeat of the near disastrous opening day at Disneyland and tried to take appropriate precautions for crowds and traffic. The Florida Highway Patrol called in 20 additional troopers to assist on the roadways, and the National Guard had two helicopters flying overhead. Disney officials opened the park hours earlier than planned when lines began to form. It turned out there would be just 10,422 park visitors for the first day and 11,115 for the second. "If the crowds were small and the traffic jams nonexistent, the enthusiasm of the visitors more than made up for it," *Orlando Sentinel* reporter Jack McDavitt wrote. One Florida family with a royal name and a sports celebrity lookalike would make history when the park opened, and one 12-year-old would have the trip of a lifetime—even though his parents weren't with him.

Facing page: Minnie Mouse, Snow White, and her seven dwarfs were among characters greeting visitors in front of Cinderella Castle on opening day.

First Day at Disney World: Not a Hitch

October 2, 1971 | Dick Marlowe, Orlando Sentinel

Disney did it. Just like they said they would.

The $400 million theme park opened more than two hours early Friday morning, climaxing six years of planning and building.

But the biggest news of the day was the things that didn't happen instead of those that did.

Traffic didn't back up to Macon, Georgia, as some predicted. It didn't even back up to Kissimmee.

Crowds didn't back up at the main entrance to the theme park and people didn't stumble over each other rushing for the 30 attractions inside.

The official crowd was 10,422, about a fifth as many as are expected at Florida Field today to watch the thrice-beaten Gators play Tennessee.

But those who came enjoyed. And enjoyed, and enjoyed.

One wide-eyed lady was heard to say, "It's hard to believe this isn't real," whatever that means— but it did seem apropos in the make-believe land that includes Fantasyland; Adventureland; Frontierland; Main Street, U.S.A.; and Liberty Square.

Another gray-haired lady leaving the theme park via one of four sleek monorails said of the fiberglass fantasy, "It's unbelievable."

Mrs. Les Stewart, who was visiting from Erie, Pennsylvania, added, "We're coming back next year and bringing four granddaughters. They'll love it."

The crowd, which came early and stayed until security hosts cleared the park at 6:00 PM, strolled casually beneath the hot sun choosing the inside air-conditioned shows over the outside attractions.

The top attraction Friday appeared to be the Hall of Presidents, which played to a full house time and again. Just around the corner at the Mickey Mouse Revue, the attraction went on at 4:30 with more than two-thirds of the seats empty.

Also a big hit was the Country Bear Band with stupid-looking "Big Al" stealing the show with

Above: Kim Buetti of Miami waits for the gates of the Magic Kingdom at Walt Disney World in Orlando to open on October 1, 1971. Facing page: A fife and drum corps parade through Liberty Square in front of the Hall of Presidents. The patriotic annimatronic attraction was one of the most popular among the first visitors to the Magic Kingdom.

Opening Day Finally Arrives

DISNEY WORLD *at 50*

The sounds of this marching band on Main Street, U.S.A. greeted the first visitors to the Magic Kingdom.

Opening Day Finally Arrives

his rendition of "Blood on the Saddle." Rookie attendants at "It's a Small World" kept their smiles throughout the busy day as they ushered thousands aboard boats for a trip through a fun-filled tunnel of color, sounds, and movement—all reflecting happiness.

Attendants on some of the attractions stood almost idle as the crowd passed up such things as the "Mad Tea Party" and "Mr. Toad's Wild Ride."

But Disney officials said the crowd was just what they wanted.

Obviously, missing were the children. Adults outnumbered youngsters 10 to 1, leaving several of the child-oriented attractions with not much to do but wait for the weekend when school is out.

Peter Pan's Flight and 20,000 Leagues Under the Sea never got going. E. Cardon Walker, executive vice president and operations chief, said, "Maybe tomorrow."

Walker said he expects much bigger crowds today and Sunday. "We'll be very happy," he said, "if we get 20,000 to 25,000 for Saturday and Sunday."

Walker said October is "a month to get acquainted, to establish ourselves and to record our television show."

A 90-minute color spectacular will be filmed October 23–25 and be shown October 29.

Walker said first-day problems were minimal and "insignificant."

He also said the public will dictate operating hours for the park. It has advertised it will be open from 10:00 AM until 6:00 PM, "but if

On opening day (from top): crowds line up at 20,000 Leagues Under the Sea; an overhead shot shows Liberty Square with the popular Haunted Mansion in the upper left; a parade makes its way down Main Street, U.S.A.; and two visitors stroll by Tomorrowland.

A Dixieland band prepares to greet the first visitors at Disney World's Magic Kingdom on opening day.

the demand is different," said Walker, "we'll change it."

"If I had any regret," said Walker, "it is that a guy called Walt Disney wasn't here to enjoy it."

Walker also credited the some 6,000 employees, most of them young and inexperienced with a "remarkable job." He also said there is more to come.

"Construction is beginning for Eastern Airlines and RCA attractions," he said. "We also are giving consideration to construction of a Space Mountain. Phase I is just the beginning."

Construction also continues on Tomorrowland and the two hotels—the Polynesian Village and the huge Contemporary Resort Hotel.

Walker said the "Flight to the Moon" attraction, one of the main events of Tomorrowland, "will be ready sometime in November or December."

Roy Disney, chairman of the board for Walt Disney Productions, did not attend the opening day. Donn Tatum, president, explained, "Roy had to leave because of a serious illness in his wife's family. We are sorry he could not be here, and it is difficult to estimate when he will return."

It is a banner day for the Windsor family on their first—but not last—trip to the Magic Kingdom.

The first family through the gates as Disney World opened Friday, October 1, 1971, rides the train into the Magic Kingdom. From left are Mickey Mouse, Lee (age one-and-a-half), William Windsor Jr., Jay (age three), Marty Windsor, and Disney World ambassador Debbie Dane.

Meet the Windsors: Disney World's First Family

October 2, 1981 | David Wilkening, Orlando Sentinel

The four of them slept Thursday night in their Volkswagen, parked at a Texaco station just off Interstate 4. They dreamed of the impossible: winning a lifetime pass to Walt Disney World.

The impossible happened. Cinderella became a beautiful princess. The frog turned into a prince. The dream came true.

William Windsor Jr., his wife, and their two small children from Lakeland Friday morning were named the "first family" as Disney World opened its gates to thousands of guests.

To a family that never won a contest, it was a startling "victory." Their eyes were bright with excitement when they learned they had won.

William Windsor Jr. carries his son Lee, while mother Marty Windsor holds son Jay. The Windsors, from Lakeland, Florida, were the first family to enter Disney World's Magic Kingdom on opening day, October 1, 1971.

Windsor, a 23-year-old apartment manager-owner, and lookalike for golfer Jack Nicklaus, said: "When I was a little boy, I always dreamed of going to Disneyland.

"It's not just for myself," he said, "but for these two fellows."

His wife, Marty, responded to the news this way:

"I can't believe it. I think I'm still asleep and dreaming."

The couple's two children, both blue-eyed blonds, had nothing to say. Jay, three, and Lee, one-and-a-half, "must be too overcome to say anything," suggested their father.

The Windsor family spent the day on an accelerated tour that left them tired and sweat-stained. Asked if they wanted to rest in the afternoon, Windsor said:

"Only for a little while. We don't want to miss anything."

The Windsors, who slept in their car to be the first family in the park, are welcomed as Disney World's first family by Mickey Mouse and Disney World ambassador Debbie Dane (holding three-year-old Jay Windsor).

The family, determined to see everything Friday, was escorted by Disney ambassador Debby Dane and other Disney officials.

They were followed by dozens of reporters and photographers. The Windsors were serenaded by bands and introduced to Disney characters at the attraction. Mickey Mouse spent much of the day with them.

The Windsors almost did not come to Disney World. A friend discouraged them, saying they would never be the first family.

Windsor figured the friend just wanted them to stay home and play poker, so he packed the luggage and the kids into the Volkswagen Thursday.

When the Windsors were named the first family, some startled photographers thought they were seeing Nicklaus. So did some tourists.

Repeatedly asked if he was ever mistaken for the golfer, Windsor said:

Darkness falls on Cinderella Castle after the Magic Kindgom's first day. The castle was completed in July 1971, after about 18 months of construction and was designed to reflect the late-Gothic, flamboyant style of the 1400s.

"All the time. It happens all the time." He added he does not play golf.

The Windsors toured numerous attractions. They took a ride aboard a steam-powered train, which whistled and blew puffy clouds of smoke into the air as it carried them around the Magic Kingdom.

When the Windsors arrived at Cinderella Castle, they were greeted by numerous Disney characters. Jay and Lee waved pennants, clutched balloons and danced up and down as they were serenaded by a band playing a medley of Disney songs. One of the songs, appropriately, was "When You Wish Upon a Star."

The Windsors stayed overnight at the attraction. They were given a large key. They also received a lifetime gold pass.

Disney officials say Windsor will receive $9.50 in refund money for the two ticket books he bought before a dream came true for his family.

"I don't care," said Windsor, grinning and looking like Jack Nicklaus again. "If they don't refund my money, I won't care."

12-Year-Old Travels Cross Country (Alone) to Visit Disney World

October 2, 1971 | Orlando Sentinel

It was a zippity-doo-dah day for 12-year-old Tom Morris of Newport Beach, California, Friday.

He had a wonderful feeling as everything was going his way.

The lad, a seventh grader with a paper route, said he saved his pennies for six months to spend opening day at Walt Disney World, and by Jiminy (Cricket) he made it.

"I just thought it would be neat to come here," explained the happy youngster who surprised Disney officials with his presence.

Although unexpected, he was given the VIP treatment. "Yes, I'm glad I came. My parents gave me permission," he said, anxious to tear off to see the sights and do the rides in Fantasyland. Tom flew in from California by himself for one precious day at Disney World. It was also his first plane flight, he said.

The youth said he saved $260 from his paper route for the round-trip. For the wonderful day, he was wearing a bright smile, brown pants, a purple T-shirt and, of course, a Mickey Mouse wristwatch. A camera never left his hands.

What inspired his adventure?

"I've been to Disneyland 19 times," he said, repeating, "and I just thought it would be neat."

CHAPTER 5

Exploring the Lands of the Kingdom

How magical was the Magic Kingdom on opening day? Barbara Schulz, a housewife from St. Petersburg, had leftover Disneyland admission tickets from 1959—which Disney World gladly accepted for her family, including her husband and twin daughters. "I like the birds," chirped young Barbara Jr., in reference to her visit to the Tropical Serenade attraction. Everyone visiting Disney World seemed to have a favorite ride or place. In the days and weeks that followed the theme park's opening, *Orlando Sentinel* readers were given multiple stories about the sights to see at the Magic Kingdom.

the Enchanted TIKI BIRDS Starring in
TROPICAL SERENADE

Facing page: Julie Andrews performs in front of Cinderella's Golden Carrousel in the Magic Kingdom for the park's grand opening. Photo courtesy of Getty Images

Main Street, Liberty Square Recollect Era of "Good Old Days"

October 2, 1971 | Ann Killiany, Orlando Sentinel

It's a trip to another era, to the "good old days." It's Main Street, U.S.A. at Walt Disney World.

Trolley cars drawn by Clydesdale horses provide the transportation down Main Street, which is similar to its cousin in Disneyland, although "Florida's is much better," according to one visitor.

Every detail of the shops is exact, and costumes on the policemen on Main Street fit their stolid forms as authentically as in 1890.

It is the first real view of Walt Disney World, and the detail of the buildings and costumes has obviously been carefully researched.

Songs by a barbershop quartet is the first entertainment on Main Street. The quartet consists of Jerry Siggins, Dick Kneeland, Bob Mathis, and Bud Thomas, all imported from California. The oldest member, Thomas, has been with Disney the longest. They now make their homes here.

Another early bit of Americana is provided by a piano built into a large white tricycle. It is played by Randy Morris, another California import.

Main Street is lined with many shops, some finished, some not.

To the left of Cinderella's Castle is Liberty Square, as Colonial American as Williamsburg.

But Liberty Square also has a haunted house, which really appears to be. It's all done with mirrors.

The Hall of Presidents is a multimedia presentation and stage show featuring animatronic figures of every president of the United States.

The Hall of Presidents is an exhibit of lifelike figures which appear so human it is hard to believe they are computer-controlled.

A brilliantly costumed Drum and Fife Corps marches around the square. Again the costumes throughout the area are authentic in every detail. The visitor is in another era the minute he crosses the bridge. 🐾

Visitors converge on Main Street in Disney World's Magic Kingdom two days before Christmas in 1972.

The Swiss Family Treehouse gives visitors a tree-top view of Adventureland.

Adventureland, Frontierland Bring Dreamy Yesteryear to Reality

October 2, 1971 | Orlando Sentinel

Remember those childhood daydreams, living in a treehouse with the Swiss Family Robinson, exploring darkest Africa, canoeing with Davy Crockett, keelboating with Mike Fink?

They all came alive at Walt Disney World in Adventureland and Frontierland.

In Adventureland, you can climb the 60 feet to the Swiss Family treehouse and stare down at the crocodile-infested water below.

You can cruise down the river through primitive lands, listen to a playful elephant sing under a waterfall, challenge a snarling tiger, and explore ancient temples.

Then take a short walk and enter Frontierland and stroll among the cowhands and Indians of 100 years ago.

Don a coonskin hat and ride Davy Crockett's canoes or Mike Fink's keelboat. You'll ride past Tom Sawyer's island, past the trapper's burning cabin, past the camp of the buffalo hunters.

But the big attraction, particularly for the smaller fry, was the Country Bear Jamboree. It's a band of bears making the finest country music ever played by bears. It is true Disney. 🐭

Mike Fink's keelboat (above). George McGill (below) helps riders onto a Jungle Cruise river boat in Adventureland on June 29, 1979.

Fantasyland Just That; Tommorrowland Is "Coming"

October 2, 1971 | Jean Yothers, Orlando Sentinel

Fantasyland is fascinating. Tomorrowland promises to be.

Bats fly. Open-jawed crocodiles are just a snap away. Ravens screech. Owls hoot. Witches with warts on their noses cackle like something straight out of Halloween.

Visitors are in Fantasyland in Walt Disney World's Magic Kingdom, taking a two-and-a-half-minute trip through the Seven Dwarfs' diamond mines in "Snow White's Adventure," and it's dark and spooky. And fun.

The Mickey Mouse Revue was another crowd pleaser on opening day. A half-hour tale tracing the history of Mickey from 1928, it is a cartoon delight, bringing 86 of Walt Disney's famous characters into a musical concert of memorable Disney songs.

For another adventure, young and old alike choose an aerial journey with Dumbo, the Flying Elephant.

Tomorrowland is just a high-ho, high-ho away.

Construction crews are still whistling while they work in this fascinating section of the 100-acre theme park, and Tomorrowland was available only as a walk-through area.

Meanwhile, visitors are able to view the site by looking from the overhead Skyway, a thrilling sky-high journey in little gondolas carrying passengers from Fantasyland to Tomorrowland, the only conveyance of its kind to make a 40-degree-angle turn, according to a tour guide. 🐭

Cinderella's Golden Carrousel Has Patriotic History

November 21, 1971 | Orlando Sentinel

The golden age of carousel making is gone, but at Walt Disney World's Magic Kingdom, one of the most magnificent of all carousels from the past has been reborn.

They called her

An aerial view of Disney World on Opening Day, 1971

"Liberty" when she was created in the wartime America of 1917, this product of a proud and ancient art.

Redesigned by Disney, "Liberty" emerges as Cinderella's Golden

Carrousel, centerpiece of a medieval courtyard in Fantasyland. The carousel wears a gold-and-white canopy inspired by the tournament tents of the Crusaders.

Around the outer facing of the canopy, artists at the Walt Disney Studio have hand-painted 18 separate scenes from the Disney motion picture *Cinderella*. Each scene is approximately two feet by three feet, and taken together, tell a capsule story of *Cinderella*.

Instead of its original 73 horses, the new carousel has 90 galloping steeds, each different and each a proud tribute to the ornate detail of hand-carved ornamentation.

"Liberty" was one of the largest carousels ever made, some 60 feet in diameter. It was first built for the Detroit Palace Garden Park (long since gone and forgotten by most). Brought back to her Philadelphia birthplace and rehabilitated in 1928, the carousel began a 39-year reign at Olympic Park in Maplewood, New Jersey.

When the Maplewood park closed, Disney scouts were able to acquire the antique masterpiece. 🐭

The Mad Tea Party ride at Disney World's Magic Kingdom opened in 1971 without a roof. The covering was eventually added in 1973 (along with the central teapot) due to Florida's extreme weather conditions.

Cinderella Castle: Grander Than a Princess Could Imagine

November 21, 1971 | Orlando Sentinel

The dominant structure of the theme park, Cinderella Castle is more than 100 feet taller than Disneyland's now famous castle—more graceful, with slender towers, lacy gold filigree, and a total feeling of light-hearted fantasy.

Where the Disneyland castle's main inspiration came from English and German palaces, Cinderella's design goes back more to France, where the famous story originated.

French royal architect Charles Perrault first set down the story of the Glass Slipper in his classic French fairy tales volume 300 years ago.

Unfortunately, he neglected to describe his princely hero's palace.

Researchers at WED Enterprises Inc., the Disney architectural, engineering, and design firm, turned to all the famous palaces of Perrault's day—still showplaces of Europe.

Their design emerges as a romanticized composite of such royal pleasure courts as Fontainebleau, Versailles, and a dozen famed chateaux of the Loire Valley.

These and many others combined with original Disney designs prepared 20 years ago for the motion picture production of *Cinderella* have gone into the complete design.

Ten spiraling towers up to 90 feet in height above the castle keep were pre-fabricated near the site, slated, gilded, and hoisted into place.

Statuary, intricately carved columns, and grinning griffins (the medieval combination of lion and dragon) were sculpted by WED artists to guard the entrance to King Steffan's Banquet Hall.

Visitors can travel to the parapet-level restaurant on two of the six elevators in the castle, then dine beneath a stained-glass dome in an atmosphere of old world royalty. 🐭

Opening Day Attractions at Walt Disney World

1. Cinderella's Golden Carrousel—Fantasyland
2. Country Bear Jamboree—Frontierland
3. Davy Crockett Explorer Canoes—Frontierland
4. Diamond Horseshoe Revue—Frontierland
5. Dumbo the Flying Elephant—Fantasyland
6. Frontierland Shootin' Gallery—Frontierland
7. Grand Prix Raceway—Tomorrowland
8. Hall of Presidents—Liberty Square
9. Haunted Mansion—Liberty Square
10. It's a Small World—Fantasyland
11. Jungle Cruise—Adventureland
12. Mad Tea Party—Fantasyland
13. Main Street Vehicles—Main Street, U.S.A.
14. Main Street Cinema—Main Street, U.S.A.
15. Mickey Mouse Revue—Fantasyland
16. Mike Fink Keel Boats—Frontierland
17. Mr. Toad's Wild Ride—Fantasyland
18. Penny Arcade—Main Street, U.S.A.
19. Skyway—Fantasyland
20. Snow White's Scary Adventures—Fantasyland
21. Swiss Family Treehouse—Adventureland
22. Tropical Serenade—Adventureland
23. Walt Disney World RailRoad—Frontierland

Operating Shortly After Opening Day

- Admiral Joe Fowler Riverboat—Liberty Square
- America the Beautiful—Tomorrowland
- Flight to the Moon—Tomorrowland
- Peter Pan's Flight—Fantasyland
- 20,000 Leagues Under the Sea—Fantasyland

Grand Prix Raceway (top), a Tomorrowland attraction, and a submarine voyage (bottom), at 20,000 Leagues Under the Sea.

Haunted Mansion Is Gathering Place for Playful Ghouls

November 21, 1971 | Orlando Sentinel

Visitors to the Central Florida Vacation Kingdom will discover that the apparitions who have taken up housekeeping in the stone-faced Haunted Mansion are 999 of the happiest and most mischievous spirits in the world.

The mansion itself is a foreboding edifice that appears to be hovering on the banks of the Rivers of America, its menacing "early Edgar Allan Poe" architecture beckoning to scareable audiences to come inside and partake of a phantasmagoric happening.

Dating back to American Revolutionary days, when witches were burned at the stake and superstition was king, the Haunted Mansion holds forth like the Hudson River stronghold of

The Haunted Mansion was an opening-day attraction at Magic Kingdom, where it is part of Liberty Square.

Peter Stuyvesant. An active retirement home for restless spirits and spooks—its cobwebbed corridors filled with wall-to-wall running chills, ghostly wails, and clanking chains—the mansion stands at the edge of Liberty Square.

But inside the mansion, more mischievous spirits only come halfway "back to life," their unearthly state humorously transparent.

They seem to appear and disappear at will to the haunting strains of a "Grim Grinning Ghosts" theme song. Headless knights and baying hounds, a chanting head in a crystal ball, floating mummies and singing marble busts are among its immortal inhabitants. 🐭

The "Bear" Truth: Country Bear Jamboree Is Whoopin', Hollerin' Fun

November 21, 1971 | Orlando Sentinel

Even Goldilocks—cold porridge notwithstanding—would love the bears at Walt Disney World's Magic Kingdom.

That's because never before in the history of show business has such a conglomeration of cavorting, carefree carnivores engaged in such

The Country Bear Jamboree in the Magic Kingdom at Disney World is a stage show with audio-animatronic figures.

frantic, furry frivolity and madcap, mirthful merriment.

The "bear" truth is that this is the zaniest troop of musical performers ever to set paws on a stage… and they're all a whoopin' and a hollerin' in a raucous welcome to visitors at the Magic Kingdom theme park. Only the Disney imagination could conjure up such an obstreperous contingent of frustrated hams as the 18 bears—not to mention a raccoon, buffalo, stag, and moose—who star in the Country Bear Jamboree.

And only the electronic wizardry of the sophisticated Disney "Audio-Animatronics" system could bring the musical bears and their funnybone-ticklin' friends to life with such believable and entertaining realism. 🐭

Technology, History Mixed for Hall of Presidents

November 19, 1972 | Orlando Sentinel

The Hall of Presidents dramatizes in a different and exciting way the importance of America's heritage, the Constitution, and the presidency.

More than 15 years in conception, design, and execution by WED Enterprises, the Disney "Imagineering" division, the Hall of Presidents represents painstaking research and is the most dramatic and prestigious show in Walt Disney World's Magic Kingdom.

Sculptors spent two years creating life-size figures of all 36 presidents, from Washington through Nixon. Authenticity is the keynote of the Hall of Presidents show, from furniture on stage to wigs, jewelry, and costumes worn by the "stars."

The chair in which George Washington sits, for example, is an exact reproduction of the chair in which the "Father of His Country" sat during the 1787 Constitutional Convention.

Extensive and exhausting research and painstaking skill are woven into the presidential wardrobe, designed by Disney artists and created in cloth by two veteran Hollywood film tailors.

The pair meticulously hand-tailored each costume, reproducing not only the style of suit worn by each president, but using sewing techniques and styles of cutting and stitching in vogue during each period in history. 🐭

Facing page: Visitors watch the Hall of Presidents show on February 6, 2006. Above: Tailors prepare the clothing for the Hall of Presidents in 1971.

CHAPTER 6

Transportation Around the World

Even the modes of transportation for Disney World were going to be attractions unto themselves. Visitors arriving via trams at the Transportation and Ticket Center could choose old-fashioned or new-fangled ways to travel across or around the Seven Seas Lagoon to get to the Magic Kingdom. And once in the theme park, guests could take a ride on a real piece of history, saved years earlier from the jungles of the Yucatan Peninsula.

Facing page: The Walt Disney World Railroad opened to the public for the first time on October 1, 1971, the same day that the Magic Kingdom park opened. Its route is 1.5 miles in length and encircles most of the park, with train stations in three different park areas.

Monorails Transport Visitors in Futuristic Style

November 21, 1971 | Orlando Sentinel

Monorails have been the rapid transit dream of city planners for years.

Monorail trains at Walt Disney World, running over a three-and-one-half-mile course, are the longest regularly scheduled monorail system in the world.

The system carries passengers on concrete beams running in either direction from a transportation center on the edge of a 12,000-car parking lot at Disney World.

Soaring up to 60 feet above ground as it crosses a ship channel between Bay Lake and the lagoon, the concrete highway in the sky passes directly through the huge lobby-concourse of the Contemporary Hotel.

It stops in front of the theme park and beside the Polynesian Hotel on its return to the transportation center. As three other theme hotels are completed, monorail service will be extended to the hotels and other recreation facilities.

Each train is air-conditioned and capable of full operation in either direction, attaining speeds up to 45 miles per hour.

Disney World's new monorails (above) leave the Martin Marietta Corporation in Orlando where they were built as part of a $1 million deal. A monorail stop (left) at the Polynesian Hotel.

When all six trains are in operation, they can handle 8,500 passengers an hour.

The first monorail trains were put into operation at Disneyland in California in 1959. Additional trains were added in 1961, and new models added again last summer.

Monorails at Disney World were constructed in Orlando by Martin Marietta Corp. involving a $1 million contract for six trains, each with a capacity for 212 passengers. Two more trains are planned.

What does a Walt Disney World monorail use for transportation? In this case, it was a tractor trailer—used to transport the new monorail to the Magic Kingdom.

History Rides the Rails on Disney World Railroad

November 21, 1971 | Orlando Sentinel

Three old, wood-burning, fire-breathing locomotives from Mexico's Yucatan Peninsula—all built shortly after the turn of the century—have taken their place in Walt Disney World's theme park to carry millions of guests in open-sided railroad cars around the Magic Kingdom.

The locomotives, found in a train hunt by a team of Disney railroad scouts, were rehabilitated—in of all places—a converted ship repair building on the shore of Tampa Bay.

With a welding torch as a magic wand and the Disney technical, artistic, and imaginative know-how as props, workers transformed the once smoke-blackened and shabby locomotives into "works of art."

The oldest of the steamers was built in 1902 by the Baldwin Co. of Philadelphia. The other four are of 1915–1928 vintage.

Removable parts, particularly the brass bells and water pumps, were stripped from the engines before their trip to Florida, riding the rails on flatcars up to Texas, across to Jacksonville, and down the coast to Tampa.

That was more than a year and a half ago. Since then, each of the five engines has completed its mechanical face-lifting, wearing many new custom-made parts.

Three of the locomotives—each about twice the size of the locomotives at California's Disneyland—puff along the track in the Magic Kingdom, each capable of pulling five passenger cars with a total passenger capacity of 300.

The passenger cars were fabricated from scratch in the same warehouse where the locomotives were renovated. The trains travel around the Magic Kingdom on a one-and-a-half-mile-long track, the same kind of narrow gauge track—three feet wide—that they traveled on in Mexico.

When visitors to the Magic Kingdom board the steam-powered trains, they will never guess that the brightly painted locomotives with their gleaming brass decorations once strained over rock roadbeds through the wild jungles of southernmost Mexico more than half a century ago. 🐭

On May 15, 1971, Mickey Mouse greets Earl Vilmer, the man responsible for purchasing the steam locomotives for Disney World and Disneyland.

Disney World Has the World's Ninth-Largest Navy

September 17, 1971 | Orlando Sentinel

It's "Anchors Aweigh" in the heart of Central Florida, where approximately 200 unique and colorful watercraft in the Walt Disney World Navy are taking their place on waterways in the Vacation Kingdom.

The world's "ninth-largest navy," with vessels ranging from sidewheel and sternwheel steamboats to canopied jungle launches, Indian canoes, keel boats and 19th-century submarines, is being made shipshape to handle more than 10 million visitors expected during the first year Disney World is open.

Ships in the Vacation Kingdom Navy will play important entertainment roles in the new Magic Kingdom theme park and vital parts in a transportation network linking Disney World's resort hotels and recreation sites with the park.

The first boats to be completed were 16 Adventureland Jungle launches, a new version of the craft used on one of the most popular attractions in California's Disneyland.

Similar in appearance but larger and equipped with steam power are six transportation launches. The 38-foot launches belonging to a new "Voyager" class will carry 35 passengers each across Bay Lake and the Seven Seas Lagoon from hotel and recreation sites and the main guest boarding area to the theme park entrance.

The most important transportation watercraft in the fleet are two new sidewheel steamboats patterned after Florida river craft of 100 years ago.

The Osceola-class sidewheeler steamboats, called the Southern Seas and Ports O' Call, each will carry 200 passengers from the main parking area to the theme park. They will also be used for moonlight cruises on the 650-acre lake-lagoon area in the heart of the Vacation Kingdom.

Flagship of the Disney World Navy will be a new Mark Twain class, a stern paddlewheel steamboat similar to its Disneyland counterpart. The new Mark Twain will carry 450 passengers along the Rivers of America in the Magic Kingdom.

Acknowledged commander of this unusual new navy is Admiral Joseph W. Fowler, U.S.N., (ret.). Appropriately the new sternwheeler bears the name *Admiral Joe Fowler*.

Since joining Walt Disney in 1954, Admiral Fowler has been in charge of all Disneyland construction and currently is senior vice president in charge of construction for Disney World. 🐭

Visitors enjoy a ride on the Admiral Joe Fowler.

CHAPTER 7

The Magical Places to Stay and Play

One of the major differences between Disneyland and Disney World was that the Orlando attraction was envisioned as a "Vacation Kingdom" with a variety of recreation and resort facilities for family fun and relaxation—themed resort hotels, championship golf courses, wilderness campgrounds, lakes, streams, and trails. The ultra-modern Contemporary and the exotic Polynesian were the only two of the first five planned hotels to open around Disney World. Ideas for hotels themed as the Venetian, the Persian, and the Asian would be scrapped. But that didn't seem to deter Disney World's first visitors.

Facing page: The inside of the Contemporary Hotel is much like an outdoor park—but with an always comfortable, air-conditioned climate.

The Magical Places to Stay and Play

Contemporary Resort Hotel Full of Innovations

November 21, 1971 | Orlando Sentinel

The 1,057-room Contemporary Resort Hotel at Walt Disney World could make other hotels obsolete in terms of guest appeal.

The hotel's basic building blocks—the completely assembled unitized steel-framed rooms—share revolutionary status with other innovations—the distinctive A-frame, the cable suspension system, the gigantic space frames, and the incorporation of the monorail into the design.

The project consists mainly of a 14-story hotel structure containing public areas, banquet rooms, kitchens, hotel rooms, and restaurants plus various three-story-high annex buildings containing additional hotel rooms.

The high-rise structure is approximately 184 feet high, 220 feet wide at the base, and 468 feet long. Major convention and exhibit facilities combine with outstanding restaurants and entertainment areas, shops, nightclubs, beaches, and marina. Its two main ballrooms, the Ballroom of the Americas with 1,250 seats for diners and the Grand Republic ballroom with 950 seats, will be used for conventioneers in the lighter tourism months and for vacationers during summer and winter tourist seasons.

The Contemporary tower is one of the world's most unusual buildings in many ways.

The pre-assembled room units overlook an inner-concourse so vast it is called the "Grand Canyon"—nine levels high and 50 percent longer than a football field.

The concourse is much like an outdoor park indoors. At its center is a four-sided tile mural nine stones high depicting the colors and patterns of the Grand Canyon and its people.

Through the heart of this busy concourse travels "the silent, all-electric monorail carrying guests to the Magic Kingdom, to the main parking area, and to the Polynesian Village.

Graceful twin monorail beams encircling the 200-acre Disney World lagoon provide both local and express service. 🐭

Since Disney World's opening, the Contemporary Resort has been the flagship hotel for the "vacation kingdom."

Visitors enjoy a luncheon at the Contemporary Resort. The hotel's restaurants are among the most memorable at Walt Disney World.

Polynesian Village Offers Unique Experiences

November 21, 1971 | Orlando Sentinel

A South Sea hotel with outriggers, hula dancers, and nighttime Tiki torchlight ceremony is all part of the new Polynesian Village.

Beneath palms on the shores of the Seven Seas Lagoon, guests reside in longhouses, swim in tropic pools, and enjoy shopping, dining, and entertainment facilities.

Architecturally resembling a royal Tahitian assembly lodge, the hotel's landmark is the Great Ceremonial House. Its open lobby, offices, shops, and meeting rooms surround a central atrium with towering palm trees and cascading waterfalls. Natural sunlight comes in through a third-story skylight, topped by a peaked roof of massive Tahitian timber beams.

The Great Ceremonial House is the center of banquet and meeting areas the Melanesian, Polynesian, and Micronesian rooms and an array of shops uniquely Polynesian.

Main entertainment and dining areas are located just across the bridge from the Great Ceremonial House in a unique Outrigger building.

There in the second-story main dining area, guests may relax in the French colonial atmosphere of the Tambu Lounge and Papeete Bay Verandah. Decor captures the Verandah's Tahitian setting, overlooking the island-dotted lagoon. Both Continental and Polynesian cuisine are featured on the restaurant's Bill of Fare.

Evening entertainment at this unique Walt Disney World resort-hotel begins at dusk when island drumbeats signal runners to begin the traditional South Sea torchlight ceremony. The torchlight ceremony is part of the Polynesian dining atmosphere for frequent luaus on the hotel beach.

Guests are treated to a feast of tropical delicacies while Hawaiian guitars and swaying dancers provide an evening of entertainment. Some of the swaying dancers may even be guests themselves, after sampling the hula lessons conducted daily at the hotel poolside.

A fleet of outrigger canoes heads up the variety of sailing vessels docked at the hotel's Papeete Bay

The unique design of the Polynesian stands out at the Magic Kingdom, including the hotel's Great Ceremonial House (left). A variety of watercraft can be found at the Polynesian's Papeete Bay marina (middle). The Polynesian's tropical theme and South Pacific flair have proven to have timeless appeal.

marina. Pedal boats, paddleboats, sailboats, and ski boats also are available for water sports.

Swimmers may choose between a white sand beach or the hotel's unique pools. Equipped with a waterfall and stepping stones, the main freeform swimming pool provides a tropical setting for outdoor fashion shows, as well as lounging and dining. A wading pool caters to small children. 🐾

Fort Wilderness Offers Camping in Style

November 21, 1971 | Orlando Sentinel

Still another major vacation attraction is located on the south shore of Bay Lake.

The 600-acre Fort Wilderness camping area has campsites nestled among pines and along winding waterways.

Utility hookups, frontier store, and recreation centers are among Fort Wilderness facilities. Nearby is a private beach and horseback riding at the Tri-Circle D Ranch with miles of woodland trails.

Other facilities include picnic grounds, bicycling, and four and one-half miles of white sand beaches. The lake and lagoon also offer water skiing, fishing, swimming, and sailing.

Parades, water-staged spectaculars, nighttime fireworks, and holiday extravaganzas will be added to complete the total entertainment concept. 🐾

Disney's Fort Wilderness Resort & Campground in 1972.

Jack Nicklaus accepts the trophy from Mickey Mouse after winning the first annual Walt Disney World Open Invitational in 1971, played on the Palm and Magnolia courses at Disney World.

Anybody for Golf? Disney Has Courses Ready to Play

October 2, 1971 | Orlando Sentinel

You don't have to stay to play.

Both Walt Disney World golf courses are ready for play and open to the public.

Jack Lindquist, Disney World marketing director, said, "This might be a good time for the public to come out and play the courses since the hotels aren't in full swing yet."

The courses, sculptured by golf course architect Joe Lee out of the Central Florida wilderness, are the Palm and the Magnolia. Both play at about 6,900 yards for regular play but can be stretched out to 7,200 yards for tournaments.

Lindquist said greens fees are $10 with mandatory electric carts at $5.

"Just call Disney World… and ask for the pro shop," said Lindquist. "Golf pro Bubber Johnson will give starting times both for the Palm course and the Magnolia."

Sandy Quinn, assistant marketing director, said guests will get preferred treatment when the hotels go into full operation.

"We have to accommodate the hotel guests first," said Quinn. "We won't know until we get a little experience as a yardstick on the golf courses. If we can, we will have starting times for the public, but the hotel guests come first."

The Magnolia Course was christened early Friday morning. Promptly at 8:00 AM, the first foursome teed off. The Magnolia also will be the home of the $150,000 Walt Disney World Open December 2–5.

Sam Hamel, who designed the electrical energy plant for Walt Disney World, played with Chuck Myall, Don Edgren, and Fred Hope, all Disney employees.

Hamel was the only member of the foursome to par the first hole, a par 5. 🐭

The courses are challenging, as Nicklaus found when he missed a putt for eagle on the No. 14 hole at the 1972 edition of the tournament. Photo courtesy of AP Images

CHAPTER 8

Meet the People of the Theme Park

Audio-animatronics can only go so far in creating the wonderful world of Disney. It's the park's cast members—those in the public eye as well as those working "backstage"—who really make Mickey's magic work. There were 6,000 to 7,000 Disney World employees when the park opened in 1971. Some were drawn to Central Florida with dreams of working at the theme park, and many were rewarded with wages of about $2 an hour—and they were happy to earn that amount. Jobs ranged from sweeping cigarette butts off streets to performing as Disney characters to shepherding visitors as Hostesses. Getting all employees in the right costumes and at the right places for their jobs was no easy task.

Facing page: The Disney World ambassador finalists from 1973.

There's a Busy World Underneath the Magic Kingdom

October 2, 1971 | Bill Dunn, Orlando Sentinel

Sleepy, Sneezy, and Grumpy are arguing about press relations.

"You can quote me but only as Sneezy," Sneezy is telling a reporter. "But don't use my real name."

"No," yawns Sleepy, "you can use our real names as long as you don't give away our roles."

"That's not right at all," Grumpy in grumbling now. "Just tell it like it is, man."

As the interview is about to begin, the dwarfs' supervisor ambles up to clarify the policy: "The dwarfs aren't allowed to grant interviews at all," he says.

The reporter moves on.

As the dwarfs are resting on a cool, concrete floor, Snow White, no doubt, is resting elsewhere in the eight-acre basement beneath the mammoth Walt Disney World Theme Park.It is here where the cast of Disney characters, hostesses, and guides checked in early in the morning and were fitted and issued costumes.

Later, between parades and performances, they retreated here 50 feet underground for a moment's relaxation, costume alterations, cold drinks, air-conditioning, and to discuss such matters as the press relations of dwarfs.

To the left of the dwarfs there is a door and a sign that says: MALE ZOO DRESSING DEN. Inside, on a bulletin board, there is written on the master schedule: "MICKEY MOUSE, MINNIE MOUSE & DONALD DUCK, Main Gate at 8:50; DUMBO, lunch at 1:40; PLUTO & GOOFY, Main Gate at 2; PINOCCHIO UNIT, parade at 5:30."

It is midmorning and a young, bushy-headed lad dressed in a bright turquoise pantsuit is red-faced. And lost. The Disney basement consists of nearly 11 miles of nondescript tunneling.

The young man is perplexed. A supervisor has just told him to get a haircut before climbing the three flights of stairs to his post. But where is a barbershop?

This is where 21-year-old blonde Terri Barnes from Kissimmee comes in. She is sitting in a folding chair at the corner of Tunnel C and Tunnel D. When the Disney campgrounds open in November, she will be a recreation hostess.

But today, she has been placed at the tunnel intersection to help lost employees find the light at the end. Behind her on the wall is a huge map of the complex catacomb. Somewhere on the map, there is a barbershop.

The lad is one of 25 lost employees Terri has helped so far and it is only 10:00 AM.

Two dozen breathless residents of Pinocchio's Village can't find the tunnel to it. Later, some dwarfs stop. They can't locate Snow White. "You have to get lost down here, some way or another," explains Miss Terri. 🐭

Disney World tour guides walk in the tunnels beneath Cinderella Castle at the Magic Kingdom in 1971.

Even Street Sweepers Smile as They Work

October 5, 1971 | Dick Marlowe, Orlando Sentinel

He was a slender young man, smiling as he swept cigarette butts from beneath a table at a sidewalk cafe in Walt Disney World.

The bubbling street sweeper was George Burgess, who took a wild goose chase from New York City last month and caught the goose.

George is one of the behind-the-scenes employees at the vast Vacation Kingdom.

George gave up a job at a Gotham City East End apartment house where he was making $3.60 an hour for opening a door.

When he arrived in Orlando, he had shoulder-length hair à la Tiny Tim. George's only regret about his new job is his hair is now trimmed and short.

Financially, George says he makes out as well in Orlando on $2.05 an hour as he did in New York for $3.60. But the hair thing bugs him.

"It's really great here at the park," said George. "Everybody understands."

George and Don Smith, another Disney employee, share a room for $100 a month. They both like the area and plan to stay.

A security guard directs a prospective employee to the Disney Employment office for a preliminary interview in June 1971.

Steve Brooks has a background as different from George's as Frontierland is from Fantasyland.

Steve, 18, heard about Disney World while cooking hamburgers at a rodeo show in Cheyenne, Wyoming. He was making $1.25 an hour selling hamburgers to cowboys and he doesn't miss one minute of it. What he does miss is snow.

Sweltering under a 91-degree sun, Steve said, "It sure would be nice to see a snow-capped mountain right now."

Steve is convinced he will someday be able to put down the heavy busboy tray and step into a better Disney job.

"I know we can," said Steve, "because we've been told that by people who have done it. They are our supervisors."

A 20 percent discount and a book of tickets every three months go with the job. And those who stick with it and keep their enthusiasm after a 90-day trial period have been promised a 15-cent increase, he said.

Right now, both George and Steve are well-pleased with their jobs. They agree "the pay is better than I expected when I started down here." 🐭

Cast Has to Dress for Their Roles at Disney World

November 21, 1971 | Orlando Sentinel

Some of the most unusual and exciting costumes this side of Hollywood make up the largest working wardrobe in the world, used to garb the cast of thousands at Walt Disney World.

Employees are "cast for roles," rather than hired for jobs.

The wardrobe helps bring life to six separate lands in the theme park—focal point of the 2,500-acre resort—the two resort-hotels, and other recreation-entertainment areas.

There are more than 45,000 separate costumes, plus all the appropriate accessories, to outfit the 7,000 employees who are "on stage" each day.

Every employee, including lifeguards and wranglers at the Tri-Circle D Ranch, is costumed. In fact, each employee is provided seven costumes so that they will have a fresh one each day.

Disney employees dressed in costume walk in a parade (top) and take various forms of transportation (bottom), as they welcome visitors at the Magic Kingdom on opening day, October 1, 1971.

Both hotels feature themed costuming.

At the Polynesian Village, the mood is French Tahitian. Hence, brightly colored flower prints are featured on the sarongs and casual shirts.

The Contemporary Hotel costumes carry a fabric pattern design created by Disney artist Mary Blair. Miss Blair, who also designed the nine-story-high mural in the hotel's Grand Canyon Concourse, repeated the colors of the Grand Canyon in the costumes worn by hotel employees.

A staff of 38 seamstresses keeps the clothes in good repair and conducts daily inspections of audio-animatronic shows to make sure the costumes are in perfect working order.

The total wardrobe project is a staggering logistical task. Wardrobe manager Bob Phelps estimates well over 200,000 individual items will be in the inventory. 🐭

Disney World Hostesses Guide Visitors to Park

November 21, 1971 | Orlando Sentinel

Some of the prettiest and most personable girls in the world are ready and waiting at Walt Disney World to receive leaders of government, industry, show business, and society when they visit the vacation kingdom.

They are the Disney World hostesses who have received extensive training as tour guides for the 2,500-acre vacation resort.

Selection of the girls is based on traditions that were established at Disneyland in receiving such world leaders as Emperor Haile Selassie; Presidents Eisenhower, Truman, Kennedy, and Nixon; hundreds of entertainment celebrities; and in serving as guides for the many other guests from around the world.

One of those who accompanied Walt Disney on tours is Valerie Watson, supervisor of the hostess corps.

What do she and the employment department look for in a prospective hostess?

Debby Dane was the first Disney World ambassador. The graduate of Lyman High School was a hostess at the preview center and the 1969 homecoming queen at Florida Technological University, now called UCF.

Girls must be at least 18 years of age, attractive, and should enjoy meeting and being with people.

Hostesses and tour guides should have a pleasing personality, speak clearly, and be available to work on a regular basis. The ability to speak a foreign language is a plus in the selection of candidates because of the many visitors from foreign countries coming to Walt Disney World.

Best known of the 24 original hostesses is Debby Dane, chosen from among all employees as the first Walt Disney World ambassador. She has traveled to Panama, Washington, D.C., and many other major U.S. cities. She has met governors, mayors, and with thousands of people interested in Disney World employees.

She was chosen as typifying the happy, friendly spirit of her fellow employees. 🐭

A Disney World hostess greets the first guest to the Magic Kingdom on opening day October 1, 1971. Right: Hostesses hurry along Main Street, U.S.A. on opening day.

The three finalists—
Debby Dane, Pamela
Broyles, and Joanne
Sanders—for the
post of Disney
World's first
ambassador, the
official traveling
spokesperson for
the "Vacation
Kingdom." Dane
was selected as the
ambassador of Walt
Disney World on
October 15, 1970.

The Man Who Was Disney World's First Mickey Mouse

July 11, 1972 | Tom Fiedler, Orlando Sentinel

Walt Disney's famous theme song "Fairy tales can come true, it can happen to you" is not just so many words to one Winter Park man, better known as Mickey Mouse.

Mickey (Doug Parks) Mouse, 21, was the first Disney character on the Disney World staff. A native of upstate New York, "Mickey," as Disney officials insist on calling him, settled in Winter Park with his two brothers after tiring of his job as a short-order cook.

He was training as an auto body man when his sister-in-law mentioned that Walt Disney World was looking for short people to cast in its character roles.

"It appealed to me right away," said Mickey. "I had sort of a natural ability for the job."

Doug Parks, seated between his sister-in-law Melanie and brother Lowrey, plays Mickey Mouse at Walt Disney World. Doug Parks is 4 feet, 7 inches tall and went through three "castings" before landing the role of Mickey Mouse.

Disney World ambassador Sheri Swets and Mickey Mouse take a tour of a hotel construction site near the Magic Kingdom in April 1972.

CHAPTER 9

The Star-Studded Dedication Weekend

While the Magic Kingdom opened its gates on October 1, it did not have its "grand opening" until three weeks later when a three-day-long dedication event was held and taped for a TV special. And what a spectacular weekend it was. There was an amazing World Orchestra; a 1,076-person marching band; 52,000 balloons; plus celebrities like Bob Hope, Julie Andrews, and Rock Hudson; as well as a couple of representatives from President Nixon's White House who would become celebrities in their own right thanks to Watergate. The most poignant moment, though, was Roy Disney recalling his brother Walt's dream of Disney World.

An NBC-TV super spectacular
THE GRAND OPENING OF
Walt Disney World
90 exciting minutes!

starring Julie Andrews

Glen Campbell

Buddy Hackett
Jonathan Winters

In tribute to WALT DISNEY, a special appearance by Bob Hope

Friday, Oct. 29, 7-8:30 pm NBC-TV 5

Facing page: Conductor Arthur Fiedler leads the World Symphony concert in front of Cinderella Castle for the nationally televised opening ceremonies at Walt Disney World's Magic Kingdom in October 1971.

Celebrities and Symphony Start Grand-Opening Ceremonies

October 24, 1971 | Jack McDavitt, Dick Marlowe, and Anne Killiany, Orlando Sentinel

Nearly 40,000 visitors—the biggest crowd yet—jammed the Walt Disney World turnstiles Saturday as the $400 million Magic Kingdom kicked off its three-day formal opening celebration with the arrival of a planeload of Hollywood notables.

The celebrities, including Rock Hudson, Robert Stack, Walter Brennan, and Fred MacMurray, arrived aboard a chartered jet to take part in the festivities, starting with a performance of the World Symphony Orchestra conducted by Arthur Fiedler.

On Saturday night, the orchestra played as beautifully as if its members had been rehearsing together all of their musical lives. It is unbelievable that these musicians from around the world, invited to join the orchestra only six weeks ago, could produce such music on such short notice.

Some 2,500 invited guests, forming a sea of gorgeous gowns and black tie formality, heard a program that was obviously designed not only to please all tastes, but for the pleasure of the musicians as well.

Following the introduction of symphony members, accompanied by a roll of drums,

the orchestra opened with Aaron Copland's "Fanfare for the Common Man." It was a stunning performance and it set the tone for the evening.

The composition of Shostakovich made full use of the string section and was a rousing, joyful performance.

Fiedler was in total command and had the complete empathy and understanding of the musicians with whom he worked. They added their sympathy as he wiped a tired brow. The 141 musicians were assembled from 60 countries and 26 American states at the Disney organization's behest to add a cultural and international note to the opening.

"People from all over the world are represented here," said Mordecai Rechtman of the Israel Philharmonic. "I've met many neighbors from Lebanon and Egypt whom I could never meet otherwise, or may not meet again."

And, though selections were announced about two months ago, the first rehearsal wasn't until last Wednesday—two days before the first concert. The result, according to many members, was nothing short of "amazing." 🐭

Actor Rock Hudson (top) and comedian Jonathan Winters (bottom) arrive for the Walt Disney World opening in October 1971.

Cinderella Castle takes center stage for the Magic Kingdom's three-day-long dedication ceremony, which started on October 23, 1971.

The Star-Studded Dedication Weekend

Yes, There Are Politicians, but There Is Hope, Too

October 25, 1971 | Jean Yothers, Orlando Sentinel

President Nixon saluted Walt Disney World Sunday as the Magic Kingdom's grand opening weekend whirled on with Bob Hope topping the stars mingling with more than 30,000 visitors.

H.R. Haldeman, Mr. Nixon's chief aide, presented an American Flag on behalf of the president to Roy E. Disney, board chairman of Walt Disney Productions and brother of the late Walt Disney. Also present was Ronald Ziegler, the president's press secretary.

The flag, which has flown over the White House, is the first Mr. Nixon has personally sent to anyone, Haldeman said. It will fly over Main Street, U.S.A.

Hope, world's master emcee, brought out his bag of gags as he officially opened the spectacular 1,057-room Contemporary Resort Hotel before hundreds of special guests gathered in the hotel's Grand Canyon Concourse. The fabulous Polynesian Hotel was also dedicated during the day.

Hope's rib-tickling monologue and side-splitting asides were a high point of the opening.

Florida Gov. Rueben Askew (left) and White House press secretary Ron Ziegler talk outside the Contemporary Resort before the dedication ceremonies of Disney World in October 1971.

He was funny during the portion taped for Friday's NBC television spectacular.

"It's the biggest vacation kingdom in the world," he said, adding with one of his famous half-smiles, "and just think it all started with a gentle mouse, a bad-tempered duck, and seven mixed-up dwarfs."

He described the attraction as a swamp made into a Magic Kingdom, asking slyly, "Did you ever stop and think how you relocate 8,000 angry alligators?"

Purring into the vast Grand Canyon Concourse on a sleek all-electric monorail that runs through the heart of the hotel, Hope arrived amid applause and the strains of "Thanks for the Memories," played by the Disney World official band.

Escorted from the monorail by two comely girl guides, he told them with a wink, "Wait for me in Adventureland."

The 68-year-old glib entertainer, a national resource of humor and morale booster to U.S. troops for many years, then introduced Hollywood

Actor Fred MacMurray (left), Academy Award winner Walter Brennan (center), and entertainer June Haver gather at the Contemporary Resort for the dedication of Walt Disney World in October 1971.

Entertainer Bob Hope arrives at the Contemporary Resort via the monorail for the opening and dedication of Walt Disney World in October 1971.

Glen Campbell performs at a riverboat landing for the dedication ceremonies of Disney World in October 1971.

celebrities as they stepped from the monorail and came down a stairway.

Each raved about the entertainment complex.

"It's the most bewitching place I've ever seen," praised actress Agnes Moorehead, Endora of TV's *Bewitched* fame.

"Wow!" said veteran actor Walter Brennan. "It makes me feel young again."

Excited spectators applauded each celebrity with enthusiasm, but popular actor Fred MacMurray and his pretty blonde wife, June Haver, rated the warmest ovation. 🐭

Polynesian Night Luau Thrills 1,000 Special Guests

October 25, 1971 | Dick Marlowe, Orlando Sentinel

All the gods of the Polynesian Islands smiled on Walt Disney World Sunday night in a spectacular display of color and pageantry dedicating the $400 million theme park.

More than 1,000 guests, including some of the top names in Hollywood and television entertainment, sat on the sandy beach, enthralled with the tropical excitement of a Polynesian luau complete with a torchlight ceremony, an electrical water pageant and fantastic fireworks.

A "super spectacular" burst of pyrotechnics covering the Seven Seas Lagoon wrapped up the three-hour festival and brought the elite guests to their feet with a round of applause. Fired into the clear balmy skies to the tune of "America the Beautiful," the fireworks display brought gasps,

ooohs, and ahs from the crowd.

The unbelievable electrical water pageant, featuring "fanciful creatures of the deep" display, also thrilled the crowd as the figures glided gracefully across the lagoon after being announced by "mysterious" lights in the sky aboard the Goodyear blimp.

The water pageant, headed by a fire-breathing serpent, was followed by trained seals, frolicking porpoises, a spouting whale, and several imaginary denizens of the deep. "Quite a show," said NBC's David Brinkley, one of the special guests.

"Just another typical Florida night that could never be duplicated in California," said former Gov. Claude Kirk. 🐭

Entertainers perform for a VIP crowd of more than 1,000 at the Polynesian Village as part of Disney World's dedication ceremonies in 1971.

Odds and Ends from Grand Opening Weekend

October 25, 1971 | Charlie Wadsworth, Orlando Sentinel

The $400 million Magic Kingdom began building up for today's dedication last Saturday, and it has been some kind of weekend, to say the least.

There were many, many interesting sidebars, to be sure.

Arthur Fiedler, the World Symphony conductor, had a press picture-taking appointment at 12:30 PM, which is also the starting time for one of the Main Street parades. As guests rushed to gain vantage points along Main Street, Fiedler happily accepted a ride to his meeting place aboard one of the theme park fire trucks, and even donned a fire helmet. Someone asked who the "man with the flowing mane is."

"Oh, Arthur somebody," one spectator replied. "Nope, that's Colonel Sanders," loudly proclaimed a nearby knowledgeable spectator.

It was a sentimental visit of sorts for another visitor. She is Mrs. Tom Wilck, whose own name is Tommy. She was the late Walt Disney's personal secretary for the last eight years of his life, and she sat in at the beginning of the thinking and

A special 1,076-person marching band proceeds down Main Street, U.S.A. at the dedication of the Magic Kingdom at Walt Disney World on October 25, 1971.

planning for Disney World. She and her husband live in Washington now. He is with the Small Business Administration. Is the package that is to be dedicated today what Disney had in mind? "Oh, my, yes!" she replied. "Everything is so great. I think it is just what he ordered. This is so much bigger than Disneyland, so much bigger! But Disneyland will always be my favorite," she added softly.

By the way, guests who were taken by surprise when Ray Bolger sauntered leisurely into a coffee room at the Polynesian and just as leisurely ordered lunch, would really have been startled had they been up early Sunday. Cesar Romero, an early riser, couldn't locate an open coffee shop. So he wandered into the employees restaurant and poured himself a cup of coffee, much to the delight of the employees.

There will be three swimming pools at the Contemporary Resort in addition to the clean lake waters. One is a regular pool, larger than most, but a regular sort of pool. A second is a smaller type for toddlers. And then there's one for teenagers with rock music piped in under water.

You don't dig holes at Disney World today and leave them. A crew dug a hole near the Contemporary late one afternoon, trying to check out some power lines. They left it overnight. When they returned the next morning, they discovered that landscape crews, working at a frantic pace, had come across the hole during the night and planted a tree in it. 🐭

Walt Disney's Legacy Honored with Grand Parade

October 26, 1971 | Dick Marlowe, Orlando Sentinel

Climaxing three days of dedication ceremonies, Roy Disney made it oficial Monday afternoon, putting in plain, simple language the tribute to his brother Walt, the man who had the dream.

More than 75,000 guests visited the theme park during the three-day weekend, a Disney spokesman said, adding the figure does not include the cast of more than 5,000 in the ceremonies.

Roy, brother of the late entertainment king, told some 16,000 guests in solemn tones:

"Walt Disney World is a tribute to the philosophy and life of Walter Elias Disney…and to the talents, the dedication, and the loyalty of the entire Disney organization that made Walt Disney's dream come true. May Walt Disney World bring joy and inspiration and new knowledge to all who come to this happy place…a Magic Kingdom where the young at heart of all ages can laugh and play and learn—together."

White pigeons then circled the Town Square, trailing red, while and blue streamers, signaling the start of the dedication parade.

Headed by an assemblage of antique classic cars, the one-hour march down Main Street, U.S.A. said it all for the $400 million theme park that opened three weeks ago for a "shakedown" period.

Performers in colorful costumes of the "good old days" sang "Fortuosity" as they cavorted around the Town Square and headed for the forecourt of Cinderella's Castle.

Vintage bicycles, a crimson uniformed marching band blasting out the rhythm of "Mickey Mouse," followed closely with Mickey Mouse himself beating the "world's biggest" drum.

Children watched wide-eyed as a band of musical toy soldiers circled the square followed by plumed ostriches, a steel drum band playing calypso numbers, and costumed youngsters dressed to duplicate the theme of "It's a Small World."

Following a color guard with flags from the 50 states, Music Man Meredith Willson drew spontaneous applause as his motorized cart brought him into position to conduct the 1,076-piece Ceremonial Marching Band.

With the audience waiting in hushed expectation, the gigantic band exploded with the sound of thundering drums rolling from the train station basement where the musicians waited to march.

Drawn from area high schools, the band filled Main Street as it marched, playing "Seventy-Six Trombones."

By the time the clarinet section emerged from the train station, the leading trombonists had already reached the castle forecourt where the University of Florida Symphonic Band and a 1,500-voice chorus played and sang "When You Wish Upon a Star."

The finale came with the release of 52,000 helium-filled balloons that saturated the sky with a dozen colors as they drifted quickly out of sight past the Goodyear blimp and a helicopter filming it all for the 90-minute television show to be shown Friday night on NBC. 🐭

Conductor Meredith Wilson (top), best known for writing the 1957 hit Broadway musical The Music Man, *leads a 1,076-member marching band for Disney World's dedication on October 25, 1971. Roy O. Disney (bottom) dedicates the theme park and declares that it would be known as "Walt Disney World" in his brother's honor. Facing page: The Wilson-led marching band fills Main Street, U.S.A. as seen from Cinderella Castle during the dedication ceremony.*

CHAPTER 10

How the World Has Changed

It's been said that Walt Disney World will never be finished. When the Magic Kingdom opened in 1971, there was an initial five-year development plan to continue adding hotels and attractions to the Florida property. While most of the original hotel plans were shelved, a lot of the planned attractions were added to the theme park, including the completion of Tomorrowland. Then some grander dreams came along that would make Walt Disney World that much more special.

Facing page: A view of Disney's Grand Floridian Resort main entrance, at Walt Disney World in Lake Buena Vista, June 22, 2020.

Arrgh, the Pirates Are Coming—and Everyone Is Excited

October 29, 1973 | Orlando Sentinel

The little boat drifts, forlornly, through the eerie glow of the underground river, between stony cliffs. The banshee sounds grow nearer.

Into the gloom it creeps, past forgotten ships, their ratlines still clinging uselessly. Barnacles coat ancient pilings. The forbidding caves and grottos loom ominously.

Past a raging hurricane the boat bravely bobs, and now through scenes of battle and plunder, suddenly exploding in kaleidoscopes of dazzling color.

Disney does it again. Opening at Walt Disney World December 15 and 16 will be a new super attraction, the Pirates of the Caribbean, similar to that which has drawn 45 million visitors since it opened six years ago at Disneyland in California.

A Disney spokesman said the opening will be the most important premier at the big Florida playground since the opening of Disney World itself.

Each segment of the voyage tells its own story, Rogers said. Moving through it all is Pegleg Parrot, a swashbuckling creature with his beak into everything—including a farewell admonishment to departing voyagers to "watch out for the moving gangplank." 🐭

Pirates of the Caribbean, seen here in 1974, is located in Adventureland's Caribbean Plaza in Walt Disney World's Magic Kingdom, just past the Jungle Cruise. The ride opened on December 15, 1973.

After originally being called Treasure Island, Walt Disney World changed the name of its 11-acre zoo in Bay Lake to Discovery Island. The popular attraction closed in 1999.

Nature Is the Star at Bay Lake's Planned Treasure Island

June 1974 | Orlando Sentinel

Awaiting final construction before opening early this year is Walt Disney World's Treasure Island, located in Bay Lake, just offshore from Fort Wilderness. [Treasure Island was later renamed Discovery Island.]

The 11-acre island, densely covered with natural tropical growth, will become home to exotic animals and fowl from the world over, and visitors will hike the island's trails examining each species in its habitat.

Modeled after Robert Louis Stevenson's island, it will be complete with shipwreck, fortress, and cave. Disney designers said there will be a swamp (future home of an alligator) with wooden footpaths and bridges for guests.

Disney officials are not sure how the island will fit into the attraction rotation since this is a first-of-a-kind venture and it stands removed from the Magic Kingdom. In fact, they are not even sure it will rate as an attraction.

All cages for fowl and animal life on the island will be constructed from material that appears to have been recovered from the shipwreck and cages will be designed to be as non-restrictive as possible. Exotic birds such as parrots, macaws, and parakeets in addition to monkeys will inhabit tree houses there.

Visitors will reach the island on regularly operated shuttle boats running from the Magic Kingdom, Fort Wilderness, and resort hotels. 🐭

Disney Launches Space Mountain, StarJets, Carousel of Progress

January 16, 1975 | Dean Johnson, Orlando Sentinel

After the first eight-passenger space capsules twisted and rolled through Walt Disney World's version of outer space Wednesday, someone said, "You know, it wasn't even very reassuring to have three astronauts aboard."

The trip through the Magic Kingdom's Space Mountain, a 183-foot-high mound of concrete is a hair-raising roller-coaster ride.

The Carpenters and the Coopers were right behind them, along with Robert W. Sarnoff, chairman of the board of RCA, presenters of the attraction.

"Jim was ready to go again," Irwin said of his son, after the ride. "But I'd just as soon wait."

The dipping, breathtaking trip, he said, "accelerates somewhat less" than the real thing.

Views of Space Mountain under construction in Disney World's Tomorrowland from 1973 to 1974. Facing page: Balloons are released from Space Mountain for its opening day on January 15, 1975.

Astronauts James Irwin, Scott Carpenter, and Gordon Cooper were as secure as they would have been if NASA had been running the show.

Irwin, the lunar module pilot of Apollo 15 and now head of the spiritual High Flight Foundation in Colorado, boarded a Space Mountain capsule with his wife, Mary, and 12-year-old son, Jim.

Cooper, who blasted off from Cape Kennedy in Mercury 9 and Gemini 5, was impressed with "the way the audio and visuals' tied together," but his wife, Susan, could only say, "My knees are like Jell-O" when she was "back on Earth."

Carpenter, who made the second U.S. orbital flight aboard Mercury 7 in 1962, said the trip was "great fun."

Visitors wait in a long line (right) to ride
Space Mountain on the attraction's opening day.

The astronauts got their preview ride of Space Mountain in midmorning before the 2:00 PM official opening ceremonies when about 2,000 guests were treated to music and speeches.

"We (the astronauts) have given you on Earth a precious blue jewel in the blackness of space," Irwin said. "Now all of you may enjoy the results of Disney's dream."

Space Mountain was indeed the late Walt Disney's dream, bequeathed to the "Imagineers" who have spent months planning the $15 million–plus attraction on a 10-acre site in Tomorrowland. Wednesday's dedication also embraced the official openings of two other Tomorrowland attractions—General Electric's Carousel of Progress, a free attraction featuring audio-animatronics, and StarJets, two-passenger vehicles that spin around a central pylon to a height of 80 feet.

Another Tomorrowland addition, the People Mover, will open this spring. 🐭

At the opening of Disney World's new $15 million Space Mountain attraction are (from left) Jim Irwin, astronaut James Irwin, and Robert Sarnoff, chief executive of RCA, which sponsors the attraction.

Disney Creates Shopping Village

March 23, 1975 | Pam Pulley, Orlando Sentinel

Shoppers, including one thirsty for an unusual blackberry wine and another enamored of a tiny brass Taj Mahal music box, thronged to Lake Buena Vista Shopping Village, the latest venture of Walt Disney Productions.

Opening day filled the shops with those who bought and browsed in the 180-acre, $10 million layout at Lake Buena Vista just east of Walt Disney World.

The parking lot was filled to its 641-car capacity by 11:00 AM.

Shoppers and the merely curious from Central Florida and throughout the nation roamed the tree-shaded sidewalks and checked out the 26 boutique-type shops built of weathered brick, wood, and shake siding.

Mr. and Mrs. Mark Phillips of New Smyrna Beach examined a shelf of specialty food items

A dockside view of Lake Buena Vista Shopping Village in May 1975.

Visitors enjoy the opening of Mickey's Character Shop at Lake Buena Vista Shopping Village in November 1985.

in the Gourmet Pantry. A can of stuffed cabbage sells for $1.49. "I just like to go around and look at things," Mrs. Phillips said. "I am just along for the ride," her husband added.

Kathy Davis, 18, and Lynne Zacklin, 14, of Fort Wayne, Indiana, expressed surprise at the maze of shops clustered across the lagoon from a Lake Buena Vista townhouse where they are enjoying a vacation with Lynne's parents.

"There are so many stores," said Lynne, dressed in cut-off jeans and a T-shirt. "I want to find out which is which and buy a purse, a big purse."

Lake Buena Vista Shopping Village (left). Jack Stone (right) stacks trays of finished lollipops in front a cooling fan at Lake Buena Vista Shopping Village in December 1975.

River Country Brings Ol' Swimmin' Hole to Disney

May 16, 1976 | Orlando Sentinel

Down the White Water Rapids or floating lazily in the Ol' Swimmin' Hole are just two of many adventures in store for guests at River Country, a unique new water-oriented "land" opening in summer 1976 at Walt Disney World's Fort Wilderness.

"It's everything kids ever wanted to do at the old swimming hole down by the river in the good old days, plus all the comforts for Mom and Dad so they can participate too," says Bob Allen, vice president of Resorts.

"River Country is sort of the same idea Walt Disney had for Disneyland and Walt Disney World—a place where children can play while their parents join in the fun, too."

Disney's River Country was the first water park at Disney World. Located along the shores of Bay Lake, the park was themed as a rustic, old-fashioned swimming hole. Photos courtesy of State Archives of Florida

The centerpiece of River Country, located at the edge of the Fort Wilderness Campground and Bay Lake, is the Ol' Swimmin' Hole—a private lagoon surrounded by sculptured rock, fast-moving water slides, and white sand beaches. Here the circulating water for River Country rushes down the slopes and plunges over natural rock falls and man-made adventures into the lagoon below.

Excitement lies in store at Whoop-n'-Holler Hollow, where guests roar through giant trough-shaped water slides on two separate twisting journeys. One is 260 feet and the second 160 feet from top to bottom, and both end with a plunge into the Ol' Swimmin' Hole.

On the other side of the rocky hill lies Raft Rider Ridge, highest point in River Country, where the White Water Rapids begin their swift-moving plunge. Aboard rubber rafts, riders race 240 feet down the slopes into the water far below. Beginning at a slower pace, the ride picks up speed as it descends toward a splashy ending in the Ol' Swimmin' Hole.

There's a water adventure for everyone in this unique river world. 🐭

Opulence Will Be the Key to Disney's Grand Floridian Hotel

May 29, 1988 | Vicki Vaughn, Orlando Sentinel

Walt Disney World is betting $135 million that its Grand Floridian Beach Resort, its newest and most luxurious hotel, will become a landmark resort known around the world.

The 900-room hotel, which is the first project undertaken by Disney Development Co., Disney's real estate subsidiary, is to open July 1. Disney has taken pains that the Grand Floridian, with its Victorian touches and we've-thought-of-everything opulence, will attract affluent vacationers.

Austrian-born Erich Huemer, the hotel's general manager, said, "We want to be known as a traditional resort, such as Raffles in Singapore or the Mandarin in Hong Kong," two of the world's most exclusive resort hotels.

Built on 40 acres, the Grand Floridian includes six buildings. The main building features a five-story atrium lobby with two giant chandeliers. The hotel's red-tiled roofs and cupolas complete the Victorian look.

Disney has dressed up even the hotel's most commonplace goings-on. Maids will not wheel carts from room to room; instead, they will deliver shampoo and soap in wicker baskets. But rooms will have modern touches, of course, including TV sets that can pull in the Disney Channel. Even the bathrooms will have telephones. 🐭

Disney's Nightlife World—Pleasure Is the Program on This Island

June 4, 1989 | Parry Gettelman, Orlando Sentinel

Pleasure Island is Disney's first attempt at adult nighttime entertainment, and although the buildings and decor offer trendy sophistication, it sometimes seems as if the whole place was designed by concerned elders who don't quite realize why an uptown dive is more attractive than a chaperoned sock hop at the country club.

According to Disney lore, Pleasure Island once

Walt Disney World's Grand Floridian Hotel, seen under construction (left) on March 17, 1987, opened in July 1988.

belonged to the "legendary" explorer Merriweather Adam Pleasure. All the structures were built to look as if they had once been warehouses, sail lofts, etc., and had been renovated only recently.

Very cute, but going along with all that is rather like humoring Mom when she wants to have party games at your graduation.

Pleasure Island is located on five acres next to the Disney Village Marketplace, with restaurants and glitzy clubs set along wide, shop-lined walkways. Three of the seven clubs—the Neon Armadillo, the XZFR Rockin' Rollerdrome, and the Baton Rouge—offer live music. The Comedy

Revelers ring in the New Millennium at Walt Disney World's Pleasure Island on January 1, 2000.

Warehouse features a 45-minute Disney spoof, and there are two discos, Mannequins for adults and Videopolis East for kids. The Adventurers Club is geared toward conversation and interaction with actors/waiters playing maids, butlers, and other characters in a Victorian-style establishment.

There is no charge for exploring the shops and restaurants, but to get into any of the clubs, you have to pass an entrance exam. It's relatively easy. The answer is: $14.95 plus tax.

As you'd expect from Disney, the clubs are pleasant, brightly lighted, and spotlessly clean.

Visitors walk through Pleasure Island on May 25, 2004. Facing page: T.J. Scamming, production manager of entertainment at Pleasure Island, is preparing the park for New Year's Eve blowout on December 27, 1991.

CHAPTER 11

Disney World's Other Theme Parks

The Magic Kingdom was the first, but not the last theme park for Disney's Central Florida property. Next would come Epcot, but not the version that Walt originally envisioned. Then came the Disney-MGM Studios (later renamed Disney's Hollywood Studios), a theme park many viewed as a reaction to the impending arrival of Universal Studios Florida. And finally (for now, at least) Disney's Animal Kingdom, which harkened back to Walt Disney's nature and conservation-minded films of the 1950s.

Facing page: Balloons fill the sky in front of Spaceship Earth (right) as Epcot opens to the public.

Epcot Opens: Visitors Christen Playground of Fantasy and Technology

October 2, 1982 | Charlie Jean, Orlando Sentinel

On a bright and warm day, tens of thousands of visitors Friday got a $1 billion glimpse of Walt Disney World's grandest scheme as Epcot Center opened after nearly two decades of planning and dreaming.

They christened the late Walt Disney's last and greatest dream a wonderland of fantasy, technology, and imagination such as the world of leisure has never seen.

There were hitches and some tempers flared as the Experimental Prototype Community of Tomorrow went through its paces, but Disney officials said the problems weren't unexpected.

By midmorning, cars had filled the 6,000-space parking lot and overflowed onto the grass as the crowd obviously surpassed the 10,000 or so Disney officials had predicted for the slowest day of the week in a weak tourism month.

By 5:00 PM, they said, attendance for Epcot and its neighboring Magic Kingdom had reached

35,562. They wouldn't give a breakdown between the two attractions. The Florida Highway Patrol reported no traffic problems.

Moreover, the land of Mickey Mouse appeared comparatively deserted while long lines formed at Epcot.

With trumpets blaring, man-made fog swirling, and a costumed cast of thousands participating, Disney opened its playground colossus on a morning you could cask and sell for wine.

"We are blessed to be among people who dream what can be and convert that dream into reality," said Governor Bob Graham, who headed a throng of invited dignitaries.

Hundreds of multicolored balloons and trained pigeons trailing blue and red streamers were released after E. Cardon Walker, Walt Disney Productions board chairman, hailed Epcot as an "enormous tribute to American ingenuity."

As a Goodyear blimp circled overhead and monorail trains silently came and went, Disney

Tina Slatton (above), 20, of Gainesville, is excited for the opening of Epcot on October 1, 1982. She also attended the opening of Disney World.

Guests file into the parking lot (above) on opening day. The Cason family (left) of Winter Park is surrounded by media after being named the first family for Epcot's opening.

DISNEY WORLD at 50

Opening Day ceremonies at Epcot show crowds at the main gate with Spaceship Earth and the Kodak Pavilion in background.

Disney World's Other Theme Parks

Early construction at Walt Disney World's Epcot Center (left) is shown on January 28, 1981, almost a year and a half before the park will open. Epcot's iconic Spaceship Earth sphere (right) takes shape in a February 2, 1982, photo.

officials welcomed the first family to enter Epcot—Dick and Paula Cason of Winter Park and their four children.

The Casons received a lifetime pass to Epcot and the Magic Kingdom.

After the gates opened, lines quickly formed at many attractions. Visitors waited as long as 90 minutes to visit Spaceship Earth, a swirling ride depicting the history of communication with startlingly lifelike, animated figures.

Technical problems at one time or another shut down Spaceship Earth, the Universe of Energy, and the World of Motion.

Some guests complained about long lines at restaurants and a lack of adequate transportation around the 260-acre fantasyland.

Walker said the glitches were expected, which is why Disney conducts a month-long shakedown. Disney World got off to a better start in 1971, he said, because its rides had already been proven at Disneyland, while Epcot is totally new and untried.

A glitch of another kind occurred around noon when a construction worker who had been employed at Epcot parachuted onto the grounds. Disney officials said they took no disciplinary action "because he was a good worker." But they weren't overjoyed about his entrance.

Several miles away at the Magic Kingdom, business drooped. Only 20,000 Leagues Under the Sea had a line. Most of a dozen employees interviewed said attendance was about 50 percent below normal. 🐭

Disney-MGM Studios Opens to a Full House

May 2, 1989 | Mike Oliver, Jay Hamburg, Catherine Hinman, S. Renee Mitchell, Vicki Vaughan, and Adam Yeomans, Orlando Sentinel

The stars came out, the sun made a cameo appearance, and the public mostly applauded the $400 million Disney-MGM Studios Theme Park on opening day Monday.

Occasional rain cooled off visitors in long lines waiting for attractions like the Great Movie Ride, the Monster Sound Show, or the Backstage Studio Tour. The weather, though, did not seem to

Disney Chairman Michael Eisner (center), Bob Hope, plus Minnie and Mickey Mouse join the park's official first family, the Gutierrezes of York, Pennsylvania, in walking down Hollywood Boulevard as the Disney-MGM Studios theme park opens on May 1, 1989. Photo courtesy of AP Images

dampen attendance or the spirits of the celebrity-gawking crowd, who discovered a little Hollywood in Central Florida.

"There's George Lucas," Carlo Zulueta, 25, cried before jumping up and running along Disney's art deco recreation of Hollywood Boulevard with his Mickey Mouse autograph book.

Despite the excitement, his companion, 21-year-old Kim Degarmo of Orlando, said the new park, with less emphasis on rides than other Disney parks, "isn't quite so Disney. It's much more calm here."

Dick Nunis, president of Walt Disney Attractions, said Disney officials were pleased with opening day attendance. "We expected it," he said. "It's gratifying."

Disney does not release attendance figures, but Nunis said the 4,500-space parking lot was filled with cars and buses by 9:30 AM. The parking lot reopened about 2:00 PM.

Actress Bette Midler, Mickey Mouse and Disney Chairman Michael Eisner cut the ribbon for the opening the Disney-MGM Studios at Walt Disney World on May 1, 1989.

Visitors lined up to pay $30.65 for an adult ticket to join in the excitement of the park's opening ceremonies, which were presided over by Disney Chairman Michael Eisner and entertainer Bob

Hope. After listening to a short speech introducing the park's "first family," visitors quickly headed to the shows and rides some had traveled thousands of miles to experience.

The longest wait at any attraction was 55 minutes, Nunis said, even though Disney workers cautioned some guests that waits could be as long as 90 minutes. Those waits would not occur on a typical day at the park, he said.

Visitors stopped to watch some of the dozens of live radio and television broadcasts occurring throughout the day.

Raymond Hayducka, wife Ruth, and son Patrick were beaming over their good luck. They had just seen a live broadcast of their favorite entertainers Regis Philbin and Kathie Lee Gifford.

"We watch it every day back home," said Ruth Hayducka. Back home is Bloomfield, New Jersey, where Raymond, 42, is a production supervisor for Reichold Chemical.

Indeed, the possibility of seeing a star or perhaps even being a star in one of the many audience-participation attractions at the park was to many as much fun as Catastrophe Canyon, where visitors are splashed from a flood and flashed by an explosion.

Spontaneous performances seemed to pop up everywhere: A "Keystone Kop" directed people traffic down Hollywood Boulevard; "Mama" came out of a restaurant kitchen and ordered a customer to finish everything on his plate; and a street cleaner pulled "rags of the stars" out of his trash can.

Not all of the scenes are well-planned, though. A security guard had to rush to the rescue of Donald Duck, who was mobbed by children when he appeared about noon in front of the Soundstage Restaurant.

Restaurants, especially the Hollywood Brown Derby and '50s Prime Time Cafe were popular and remained full into the evening. 🐭

Animal Kingdom Opens

April 23, 1998 | Cory Lancaster, Tim Barker, and Lesley Clark, Orlando Sentinel

The house was packed. The lines generally were short. The glitches were few. And the weather was perfect.

Could even Disney have scripted a day like this?

The planets seemed in perfect alignment as Walt Disney World opened its fourth and largest theme park to a crowd of thousands, who began arriving at the gates before dawn.

Disney's first new park in almost a decade attracted so many visitors that the 6,000-car parking lot was closed an hour after the 6:00 AM opening.

"This has just been an amazing day," Bob Lamb, Disney's vice president for Animal Kingdom, said Wednesday evening. "We're giddy at this point."

The only downside was when the park's sole thrill ride, Countdown to Extinction, closed for nearly an hour because of technical problems. And some tourists wanted more exciting rides.

Disney Imagineer Joe Rohde (left), creative director for Disney's Animal Kingdom, describes a prototype of planned theme park for Disney CEO Michael Eisner and vice chairman Roy Disney (right) in Orlando on June 20, 1995. Disney's fourth theme park would open in 1998.

The Tree of Life is growing and taking shape along with the rest of Disney's Animal Kingdom on March 25, 1997.

But the overall impression was positive.

"It's awesome," said Sara Davis, 18, of Champaign, Illinois. "There are more rides at other parks, but this is natural and relaxing and entertaining."

Disney unveiled the park on Earth Day, with the stated hope of turning a profit while entertaining, educating, and motivating people to protect the environment.

The park is a radical departure for Disney. But executives say it's a return to the company's roots, when Walt Disney preached conservation in his 1950s nature films.

The message may have been lost on first-day visitors. The buzz was rides and attractions, with the best reviews going to the safari ride, a 3-D comedy movie about bugs, and the dinosaur-themed thrill ride.

Crowds linger in front of the Tree of Life—the centerpiece of Disney's newest attraction, Animal Kingdom—during opening day on April 22, 1998.

"I would say I like this park the best," said Maureen Schneider, visiting from Haverhill, Massachusetts, with her husband and two children. "The safari ride with all the animals was incredible. Nobody should miss that."

A few said the 500-acre, $800 million park didn't quite meet their expectations. The boat ride was a little boring. The safari vehicles go too fast. And there weren't animals in all the animal areas.

"I'm not sure what I think," said Dena Morris of Bethany, Connecticut. "We've been going back and forth about that all morning."

There weren't enough rides to suit Robert and Barbara Light of Indiana. But they said they'll return next year with their two children in tow when the park's sixth land, Asia, opens with its water thrill ride. "It'll be better when a few more attractions are open," Robert K Light said.

Judson Green, Walt Disney attractions president, gives chimp expert Jane Goodall a porcelain Tree of Life on April 22, 1998, during opening day ceremonies at Disney's Animal Kingdom.

Unlike other park openings that featured glitzy Hollywood stars, Animal Kingdom's was more subdued.

Actor Drew Carey, however, attracted a crowd while filming in Camp Minnie-Mickey for Sunday's Animal Kingdom special on ABC-TV.

But like other openings, there were diehard Disney fans. At 5:00 AM, 350 cars were waiting at the parking plaza to get into the Animal Kingdom.

First at the gates were Brenda Herr, husband Damon Chepren, and their 22-month-old son. The St. Petersburg couple stayed up nearly all night, napping for two hours in a Mazda 626, to ensure a spot at the front.

Herr said she has long wanted to be a Disney park's "First Family." The honor includes theme park passes for life at Walt Disney World.

"She was determined, and she let me know darn well we were going to make it happen," Chepren said. "When we were waiting in the car, she looked me in the eyes and said, 'You will run.'"

The park was scheduled to open at 7:00 AM, but Disney let visitors through the turnstiles an hour early after a brief ceremony with the "Circle of Life" song from Disney's *The Lion King* movie and a burst of rose-petal confetti.

By the time the Kilimanjaro Safari ride opened, there were more than 1,000 people in line, stretching the length of Harambe village. The wait: more than an hour and a half.

The Tree of Life at Disney's Animal Kingdom is illuminated in the dim light just before sunrise on April 18, 1998.

"We're diehards," said Nannette Decker, who lives near Tampa. "What's Disney without lines? Especially on opening day." 🐭

CHAPTER 12

Silver Anniversary Remembered

Walt Disney World's 25th anniversary celebration was a great time to reflect on all the changes that came to Central Florida as a result of Walt Disney's dream. Part of the festivities included an extreme makeover for an iconic structure, a celebrity-filled gala and a rededication of the most magical place on earth.

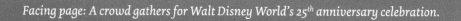

Facing page: A crowd gathers for Walt Disney World's 25th anniversary celebration.

Cinderella Castle is taking on a new hue: pink. Disney workers are changing colors as part of Walt Disney World's 25th anniversary celebration.

25th Anniversary Made to Put Disney in Pink

August 8, 1996 | Christine Shenot, Orlando Sentinel

Picture a 185-foot-tall birthday cake painted Pepto-Bismol pink and topped with white icing, gum drops, candles—the works.

In a matter of weeks, that's what Cinderella Castle, Walt Disney World's most famous icon, will look like. With the October 1 kickoff of Disney's

25th anniversary approaching, the company's entertainment and marketing teams are winding up two and a half years of preparations.

Although it will be a few more weeks before the company launches a massive marketing campaign that will ultimately involve McDonald's, the ABC network, and other big-name partners, employees have started redecorating the Magic Kingdom, the focal point of the event.

With thousands of curious visitors looking on every day, workers are painting the walls and spires of Cinderella Castle the pinkest of pinks, in the first stage of the castle's multimillion-dollar transformation into a birthday cake.

Next will come banners and other decorations on Main Street, U.S.A. "We really are completely dressing up for the occasion," said Alice Spurgeon, director of creative development and a point person on the event for more than two years.

Elsewhere on Disney property, workers are also building new archways on the roads leading into Disney World. And projects such as the new 50,000-square-foot World of Disney store under construction at the Disney Village Marketplace have been put on the fast track, racing to open in time for the start of the 15-month anniversary celebration. 🐭

Remembering How It All Started

October 1, 1996 | Leslie Doolittle, Orlando Sentinel

Uncle Walt lookalike and beloved Disney Co. vice chairman Roy E. Disney kicked off Mouse World's 25th anniversary festivities Monday, reenacting the 1965 news conference announcing the coming of Mickey & Co.

Disney shared the spotlight at Lee's Lakeside restaurant in Orlando with Gov. Lawton Chiles and E. Cardon Walker, retired president of Walt Disney Productions.

For the Magic's Kingdom's 25th anniversary, Roy E. Disney (left), Florida Gov. Lawton Chiles, and former Disney executive E. Cardon Walker recreate the historic 1965 press conference in Orlando where Walt Disney announced that he was building a theme park in Central Florida.

Among the tales shared with a packed house of Disney execs and lawmakers (including three former governors): Walker said that because the company had no idea how many people would come on opening day in 1971, he and Dick Nunis (now chairman of Walt Disney Attractions) got up early that morning and jumped into a helicopter to take a look.

Elated by the sight of a long string of car lights headed toward the park, Walker exclaimed: "Oh, boy! Here they come!"

Then they noticed the caravan was turning right. That line of cars—it turned out—was Disney employees corning to work.

Meanwhile, the ever-engaging former governor Claude Kirk Jr. said he was delighted to be invited to the reenactment: "Actually, I'm delighted to be invited anywhere these days."

Later Monday, Disney took over Orlando Arena and treated a lower bowl-full of media types from around the world (along with some local VIPs) to a star-studded show featuring song and dance, light shows, and a blizzard of confetti.

Among the stars: Brett Butler of ABC's *Grace Under Fire*, who joked to the crowd that she felt she had no choice but attend the Disney celebration because "I was afraid I'd wake up with a duck's head in my bed, or Jeff Foxworthy's." (Foxworthy's show moved from Disney-owned ABC to NBC this year.)

The celebs scheduled to be in town this week include Sharon Stone, Roy Disney, Brett Butler, Regis Philbin, Kathie Lee and Frank Gifford, the Lawrence brothers, Corbin Bernsen, Michael J. Fox, Molly Ringwald, Siskel and Ebert, Gerard Depardieu, Greg Giraldo, Bob Hope, Bob Saget, John Denver, John Tesh, Michael Eisner, Michael Ovitz, Alex Trebek, Drew Carey, Miss America Tara Dawn Holland, Daisy Fuentes, Lou Rawls, Betty White, Ed Asner, Steven Bochco, Raven-Symone, Morgan Fairchild, Paul Harvey, Bill Nye, and Angela Lansbury. 🎙

Mother Nature Rains on Mickey's Parade

October 2, 1996 | Christine Shenot and Jill Jorden Spitz, Orlando Sentinel

It was orchestrated down to every last detail: the Mickey Mouse–shaped confetti, the 1,076-piece marching band, the color-coded name tags, even the appearance by First Lady Hillary Rodham Clinton.

But there was one factor the mighty publicity machine of Walt Disney World couldn't control Tuesday at its 25th anniversary kickoff: the weather.

Though the rain subsided for much of the ceremony rededicating the Magic Kingdom, the charm wore off a few minutes too soon.

Just as a children's chorus broke into the climactic verse of "When You Wish Upon a Star," 500 white doves were released, fireworks went off, and a formation of fighter jets flew overhead, the skies opened.

Mother Nature, you might say, rained on Mickey's parade.

Still, the wet weather did little to dampen the mood of Disney officials and many of the estimated 11,000 people invited to attend the Disney World festivities, which continue through Thursday.

Facing page (clockwise from top left): Fireworks explode over Cinderella Castle, decorated as a birthday cake, at the conclusion of the 25th anniversary re-dedication ceremonies. Mickey is the star in Disney World's 25th Anniversary Parade. Magic Kingdom's 25th anniversary party featured confetti shaped like Mickey Mouse's head (above) and also rain during the Walt Disney World Celebration.

Roy E. Disney, Disney chairman Michael Eisner, and First Lady Hillary Clinton listen to the singing of 13-year-old Alberto Gruze of the Bronx as he sings "When You Wish Upon a Star" at Disney World's 25ᵗʰ anniversary celebration.

Hillary Clinton recalled her first visit to the park with her husband and their daughter, Chelsea, a decade ago. Echoing a recurring campaign theme, she thanked Disney "for making children the heart and soul of all your endeavors."

She was joined by Gov. Lawton Chiles, Disney chairman Michael Eisner, and Roy E. Disney, Walt Disney's nephew. They gathered on a stage in front of Cinderella Castle, transformed for the 15-month celebration into a pink birthday cake

Runners trot past Cinderella Castle, decorated like a birthday cake to celebrate Disney World's 25th anniversary, during the Walt Disney World Marathon on January 5, 1997.

with inflatable candles.

This being a media-driven event, Tuesday's ceremony drew about 5,000 reporters, radio hosts, and television producers. You couldn't swing a toy Goofy without hitting someone either scribbling notes, conducting interviews for a radio show, or shooting video of the much-hyped event.

Although there was grumbling about the bad seats, blocked access to certain areas, and shortage of bottled water, it seemed to be limited

Mickey Mouse opens "A Night of Magical Dreams" on September 30, 1996, ushering in Walt Disney World's 25th anniversary celebration.

to the media and special guests.

Elsewhere in the park, tourists who weren't allowed anywhere near the ceremony took advantage of shorter lines for popular rides. Others watched the event on large TV screens.

"I was hoping I could see it with my eyes," said Aleasa Hogate, 61, of Pennsville, New Jersey, who

stood on a planter and took video of the video. "Even if I had to stand in line all night, I would have done it."

But Hogate said she wouldn't have missed being in the Magic Kingdom, which she visited during its first year and on its fifth, 10th, 15th, and 20th anniversaries.

Mickey Mouse opens "A Night of Magical Dreams" on September 30, 1996, ushering in Walt Disney World's 25th anniversary celebration.

To commemorate this visit she mixed up a batch of pink frosting, which she smeared onto her wide-brimmed straw hat to create a miniature version of what Disney is calling the "Castle Cake."

Mary Beth Stabinski of Rotterdam, New York, showed similar creativity when she painted "Happy 25 WDW" T-shirts for herself, her husband, and their two children. They were hoping to catch a brief glimpse of the festivities.

"I thought it would be something special, something historic," she said of her decision to bring her kids to the park. "They may not know it while they're standing here waiting, but someday they'll thank me for this." 🐭

CHAPTER 13

Disney World: Today & Tomorrow

As the 50th anniversary of Walt Disney World arrives, the magic remains—but it exists in a very different world from just a few years ago. The coronavirus pandemic forced a months-long closure of Disney's Orlando theme parks. The NBA and Major League Soccer decided to create COVID bubbles at the Wide World of Sports, where the hometown Orlando City Soccer Club reached the championship game of the MLS Is Back tournament and the Miami Heat faced the Los Angeles Lakers in the first (and likely only) NBA Finals played at Walt Disney World.

Facing page: Guests wear masks as required to attend the official reopening of Walt Disney World on July 11, 2020. Disney reopened the Magic Kingdom and Animal Kingdom with limited capacity and safety protocols in place in response to the COVID-19 pandemic.

Disney World Closing Theme Parks as Coronavirus Concerns Swell

March 12, 2020 | Dewayne Bevil and Gabrielle Russon

Throughout its nearly 50-year history, Walt Disney World has closed briefly because of looming hurricanes and the 9/11 terrorist attacks, but late Thursday, the company announced it will shut down for nearly two weeks starting Sunday because of the coronavirus pandemic—an unprecedented move.

The announcement had a sweeping effect. About 30 minutes after Disney broke the news, Universal said its theme parks are closing Sunday most likely through the end of the month, too.

"It's truly uncharted territory," said longtime theme park reporter Robert Niles, who had earlier anticipated Disney World would follow suit after

All is quiet in the parking lots at Disney's Animal Kingdom and Magic Kingdom (facing page) as Walt Disney World enters its second week of being shut down in response to the coronavirus pandemic on March 24, 2020.

With Minnie, Mickey, and friends, Disney World president Josh D'Amaro waves to guests gathered on Main Street, U.S.A., in the Magic Kingdom in the final minutes before the park closed, Sunday night, March 15, 2020. Disney World announced that all their parks will be closed for the rest of March as a result of the coronavirus pandemic.

Disneyland, which also announced it was closing Thursday.

In Orlando, the four theme parks will shut down by the end of Sunday, but the hotels and the Disney Springs shopping center will remain open.

"In an abundance of caution and in the best interest of our guests and employees, we are proceeding with the closure of our theme parks," Disney said in a statement. "We will continue to stay in close contact with appropriate officials and health experts."

The closings of Disney World parks have been scattered throughout the resort's 48-year history. The cause has usually been hurricanes that forced operations to halt for a day or two. The theme parks were closed in September of 1999 for Hurricane Floyd and three times in 2004 as Charley, Frances, and Jeanne passed by. Matthew (2016) and Irma (2017) also prompted closures.

The parks also closed on September 11, 2001, after terrorist attacks in New York and Washington, D.C.

Disney Reopens as a Different World with Masks, Social Distancing

June 11, 2020 | Gabrielle Russon, Orlando Sentinel

Gary Semel's hands trembled in anticipation of the moment he had awaited for four months. Finally, he could kneel down in front of Cinderella Castle at Walt Disney World to propose to his girlfriend of two years, Tia Lovett, 50.

They kissed, face mask to face mask, a love story in historic times, while a Disney photographer captured the moment.

"I wanted to do it at Disney, and then it closed. I've been waiting very impatiently," said Semel, 49, turning to his future wife. "I'm sorry that I took so long. I really wanted to do it here."

Guests get their temperature taken at the Disney Springs shopping and dining district in Lake Buena Vista, June 17, 2020.

For the Jacksonville couple and many others, the return of Disney World on Saturday was a jubilant celebration. But the day brought only light crowds to the Magic Kingdom, which opened to the general public in tandem with Animal Kingdom.

Epcot and Hollywood Studios will open Wednesday as Disney's Orlando empire returns a month after Universal Orlando and SeaWorld.

Not everything was magical.

The resort's revival is happening as the coronavirus pandemic surges. The state reported 10,360 new

Guests ride the Slinky Dog Dash roller coaster after the reopening of Disney's Hollywood Studios.

Guests walk past the Millennium Falcon in the Star Wars: Galaxy's Edge land on the second day of the reopening of Disney's Hollywood Studios on July 16, 2020. All four of Disney's Florida parks had reopened after being temporarily closed for the pandemic.

coronavirus cases Saturday, the third-highest daily increase, and 95 more deaths as Florida has become one of the nation's major hot zones for the virus.

When asked why Disney was opening now, executive Josh D'Amaro responded, "We are in a new normal right now, so what's happening outside of the gates of Walt Disney World is our new world."

"We were one of the first theme parks to close, and we'll be about the last to open," he told CNN. "And we spent every minute of every day thinking about how to operate in this new normal that we're in."

At the Magic Kingdom, all Disney employees wore face coverings, and workers with high contact with guests, such as ride operators, were equipped with clear face shields as well.

Most visitors seemed to be obeying the required mask rule Saturday as well as markers meant to keep them six feet apart. Employees were observed enforcing the requirements.

"We're encouraged by our guests' overwhelmingly positive feedback for our phased

Masked visitors at Disney Springs walk by a mural featuring Orange Bird in a retro citrus add, which goes with the turn-of-the-century theme of that area of the shopping and dining complex.

reopening and are grateful for their support of the new measures we've added," Disney spokeswoman Andrea Finger said in a statement.

Bianca Jesus cried when she lined up to watch the fireworks and waved good-bye to Mickey Mouse & the gang on March 15 as Disney World, which had never closed down for more than a day or so, went dark. She wasn't alone in the outpouring of emotion.

She vowed to come back on the first day back. Jesus, a tour guide who has lived off her savings during the pandemic, booked a Disney hotel room,

even though she lives in Orlando, to guarantee advance reservation.

Her spirits were so high Saturday, she said she didn't mind wearing her mask on a hot day. She said she felt safe with Disney temperature screening visitors, the mask requirements, and seeing employees enforcing the rules.

Despite the changes from the pandemic, "it still felt like Disney," Jesus said, after snapping selfies with Winnie-the-Pooh characters who posed on a restaurant porch, spread out from guests. "I'm so grateful to be here today."

A young guest rides the Prince Charming Regal Carrousel during the official reopening day of the Magic Kingdom.

It's Time to Celebrate WDW's 50th Anniversary

February 19, 2021 | Dewayne Bevil, Orlando Sentinel

Walt Disney World has announced the first details for its 50th-anniversary celebration, which will last 18 months and include lighting enhancements to all four of its theme parks' icons, including Cinderella Castle at Magic Kingdom.

The event—dubbed "The World's Most Magical Celebration"—will begin October 1, the resort announced Friday morning. Disney World opened to the public October 1, 1971.

Expect the castle's makeover to include more gold décor. The landmark received a paint job that shifted its color scheme to deep blues and light pinks last year.

"The entire castle will shimmer with pearls and jewels, and the turrets and towers will be wrapped in iridescent gold and royal blue ribbons," said George Adams, Walt Disney Imagineering. "Above the castle gate, a 50th-anniversary crest will warmly welcome guests to join the festivities."

Epcot's Spaceship Earth, Animal Kingdom's Tree of Life, and the Twilight Zone Tower of Terror at Disney's Hollywood Studios will be incorporated into the celebration as well.

"At night, our four park icons...are going to come to life with a magical iridescent glow, covered in pixie dust, that we call the beacons of magic," said Dana Carlson, associate broadcast producer with Disney Live Entertainment.

Spaceship Earth at dusk as Epcot is readied for the upcoming 50th anniversary celebration of Walt Disney World.

What's Next for Walt Disney World?

Dewayne Bevil, Orlando Sentinel

After the 50 candles are blown out for Walt Disney World's big birthday, expect the company to unwrap more presents.

Remy's Ratatouille Adventure, a dark ride based on the 2007 Pixar film *Ratatouille*, opens at Epcot's France pavilion on October 1, 2021, 50 years to the day since Magic Kingdom opened to the public.

After that, there are more new attractions planned for Epcot, which also has an October 1 birthday, opening on that date in 1982. On tap is Guardians of the Galaxy: Cosmic Rewind, an indoor roller coaster in Future World. Disney describes the ride as a "family-friendly storytelling coaster." Its vehicles rotate 360 degrees and can do a reverse launch.

A view of the newly painted Cinderella Castle from the Seven Seas Lagoon outside the Magic Kingdom at Walt Disney World on September 30, 2020.

Cosmic Rewind and the Remy ride are parts of the much-discussed transformation of Epcot, which also includes the addition of a nighttime spectacular called "Harmonious." That show, staged on World Showcase Lagoon, incorporates five floating platforms that house fountains, moving lights, and a high-density water curtain. It replaces "Epcot Forever," which replaced the long-running "IllumiNations: Reflections of Earth."

The revamping of the entrance of Epcot features a refreshed fountain and retro acrylic towers plus new lighting built into the iconic Spaceship Earth attraction. The finished production will have Future World divided into three neighborhoods: World Celebration, World

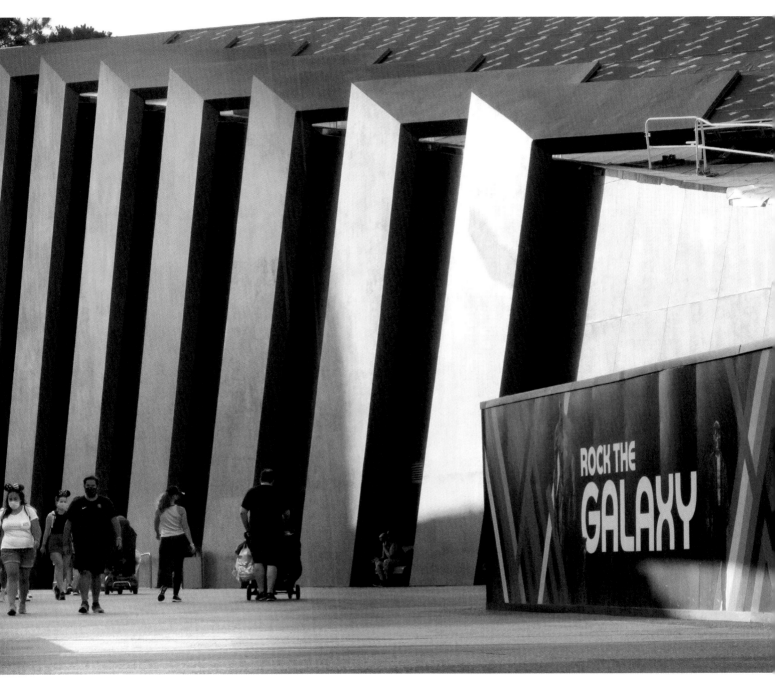

Guests walk past construction site for "Guardians of the Galaxy: Cosmic Rewind" at Epcot in April 2021 as the attraction is readied for the upcoming 50th anniversary of Disney World in October 2021. The indoor roller coaster features vehicles that rotate 360 degrees.

A topiary of Remy, the star of "Remy's Ratatouille Adventure," welcomes guests to Epcot's France pavilion, as work continues on the new ride based on the 2007 Pixar film Ratatouille in April 2021. The ride was set to open on October 1, 2021.

Discovery, and World Nature. (World Showcase—also known as "the countries"—is staying put.)

Bob Chapek, CEO of Walt Disney Co., has referred to the changes as making Epcot "more Disney, more family, and more timeless."

Another sci-fi-esque ride is coming to Magic Kingdom. TRON Lightcycle / Run, operating in Tomorrowland near Space Mountain, features fantastical two-wheeled cycles "for a thrilling race through the digital frontier," Disney says. A similar attraction debuted at Shanghai Disneyland when that theme park opened in China in 2016.

Other rides are getting updates, including Jungle Cruise, a Magic Kingdom classic that dates back to opening day in 1971, and Splash Mountain, set for a makeover to incorporate music and theming from *The Princess and the Frog.*

The company's embrace of its *Star Wars* franchise continues with a hotel experience called "Star Wars: Galactic Starcruiser" near Disney's Hollywood Studios, home of Galaxy's Edge. Not scheduled to open in 2022, plans call for a two-day/two-night all-immersive vacation with an intergalactic theme sporting launch pods and windows looking out into the cosmos.

"For the first time, adults and children alike will get to yield a lightsaber and face off against a training remote," says Ann Morrow Johnson, an executive producer with Walt Disney Imagineering.

Starcruiser visitors also will have starship tours and excursions into Batuu, the Galaxy's Edge planet.

"Guests will take an exclusive transport, and they'll emerge straight into the land," Johnson says.

Meanwhile, Disney Cruise Line is adding three ships to its fleet, starting with Disney Wish, scheduled to set sail in summer 2022.

Disney World typically is tight-lipped about opening dates and schedules. The coronavirus pandemic has only aggravated the situation. Walt Disney once said that his Disneyland would never be completed, and that philosophy has spread worldwide.

"It will continue to grow as long as there is imagination left in the world," he said. 🖤

A six-story-high structure for "Harmonious," the new show on Epcot's World Showcase Lagoon, frames part of the American Experience attraction in the distance. The new show features fireworks, fountains, and new interpretations of classic Disney songs.

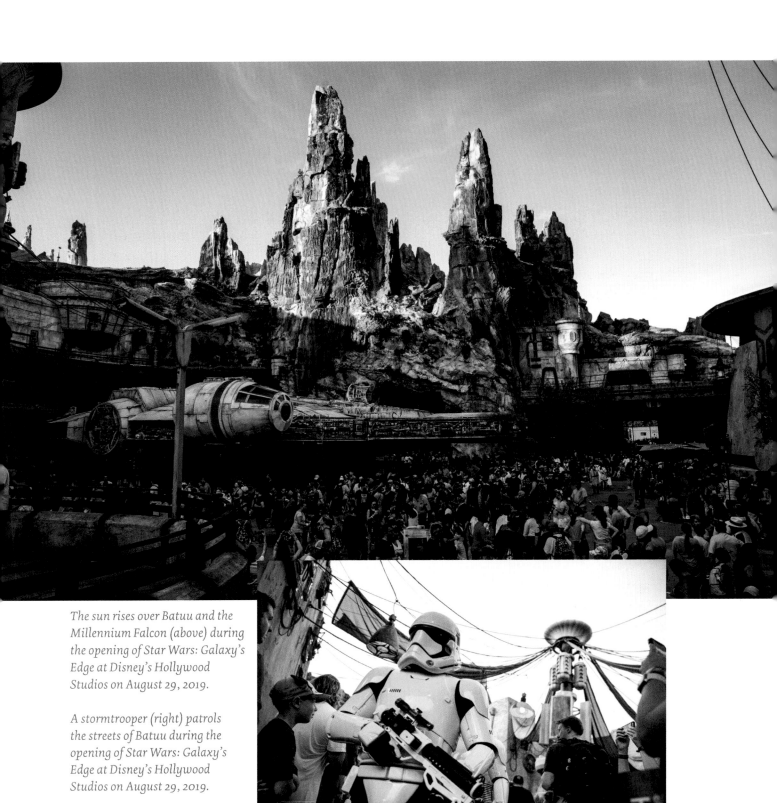

The sun rises over Batuu and the Millennium Falcon (above) during the opening of Star Wars: Galaxy's Edge at Disney's Hollywood Studios on August 29, 2019.

A stormtrooper (right) patrols the streets of Batuu during the opening of Star Wars: Galaxy's Edge at Disney's Hollywood Studios on August 29, 2019.

A view of the construction site for Tron Lightcycle / Power Run, as seen from Storybook Circus in April 2021, as the Magic Kingdom is readied for the upcoming 50th anniversary celebrations at Disney World in October 2021.

A surfer eyes the Disney Cruise Line ships Fantasy and Dream on the horizon as they sit off of Cocoa Beach, Florida, on March 24, 2021. Disney had announced a temporary suspension of sailings for their entire fleet due to COVID-19.